2

Juanita M. Kreps

LIFETIME ALLOCATION
OF WORK AND INCOME
ESSAYS IN
THE ECONOMICS
OF AGING

DUKE UNIVERSITY PRESS

Durham, North Carolina

1971

© 1971, Duke University Press
ISBN 0-8223-0249-7
LCC card number 74-161355

Second printing, 1975

PREFACE

Several studies of the social and psychological aspects of aging have emerged during the past decade. Economists have evidenced less interest in the subject, although with the onset of old age, which we are led to expect precisely on the sixty-fifth birthday, work and income arrangements are dramatically altered for most people. These changes have become highly institutionalized, making it difficult for individual differences in capacity or preference to prevail; observe that references to early or postponed retirement seem somehow to suggest abnormality of behavior.

The explanation for current retirement practice lies not in the physiology of aging but in the productivity of labor. As output per man-hour increases, man experiences higher living standards in the forms of both a greater volume of goods and services and a growth in leisure time. But whereas the increase in free time early in this century came primarily in shortened workweeks and longer vacations, events of the past two decades reveal a heavy apportionment of leisure at the end of the lifespan. The appearance of retirement as a life stage is a phenomenon of such significance to studies of income allocation as to call for a reexamination of traditional distribution theory.

The essays which follow call attention to recent developments affecting the patterns of work and earnings through the lifespan, recent and projected growth of nonworking time, levels of income by age and occupational groups, the impact of economic growth on retirement benefits, the question of optimizing the temporal allocation of work and income, and the growing role of income transfers. Some of the material presented here was published earlier by the Social Security Administration, the Joint Economic Committee, the National Commission on Technology, Automation, and Economic Progress, and the Special Committee on Aging of the United States Senate, in its hearings. Some purpose is served, nevertheless, in pulling the several strands together as a background for consideration of the broader questions of the timing of work and income.

Part of the material was prepared under a grant from the Manpower Administration, United States Department of Labor, under the authority of Title I of the Manpower Development and Training Act of 1962. Persons undertaking such projects under government sponsorship are encouraged to express freely their professional judgment. Therefore, points of view or opinions stated here do not necessarily represent the official position or policy of the Department of Labor.

J. M. K.

Durham, North Carolina

ESSAYS IN THE ECONOMICS OF AGING

IV. WORK AND INCOME ALLOCATION IN THE UNITED STATES: POLICY CONSIDERATIONS

LIFETIME ALLOCATION OF WORK AND INCOME

Joseph J. Spengler

INTRODUCTORY COMMENT: WORK REQUIREMENTS AND WORK CAPACITY

A century and a half ago, uncertainty was man's fellow traveler. Death, as Fourastié remarks, was at the center of life, and life itself was short. Man worked long hours for little, often bare subsistence. Not surprisingly, his concerns were anchored in the present. After all, he had little income and little time, present or future, to bother about, and when beset by adversity he had little chance of rising above it. His economy still was, in Patten's words, a "pain economy."

The world of which Professor Kreps writes is quite different. While it is not one in which uncertainty and chance have been replaced by certainty, it is one in which man can assume a degree of certainty, at least insofar as he accepts insurance and actuarial estimates. No doubt he thinks in terms of economizing for the future in greater measure than his ancestors, when Böhm-Bawerk commented on the systematic undervaluation of future wants. Man is aware, moreover, that his income stream has a time shape, rising over time, falling over time, rising and then falling, or falling and then rising. To this time shape, as Irving Fisher observed, man normally tends to adjust his allocation of current income between saving and consumption, which may involve also an adjustment in his distribution of time between gainful employment and leisure and other uses of time. It is of this intertemporal disposition of income, together with that of work and other applications of time, that Professor Kreps writes: how time and income are actually allocated in the course of an individual's life, and how they might better be allocated.

In the analysis of these questions of recent origin—questions which rarely existed in the days of our founding fathers and their immediate successors—it is important to note that a man who would tentatively plan the whole of his life must count strongly upon having that life in hand after, say, his tenth or twentieth year. This was hardly true of a young American even in the era of Tocqueville's visit to this country in 1831. At that time an American could be reasonably sure that he would do much the same kind of work throughout worklife, since the kinds of work men then engaged in were relatively few, and men could not shift readily from one work to another. But he could not be sure how long he would be able to work.

In earlier years, such uncertainty as to the length of time man would retain his life and health was of central importance. Around 1840 a newly born male had a life expectancy of about 40 years. More relevant, however, was his life expectancy at age 10, since at this age he would begin to look forward to taking on a self-supporting man's role. At that age, a male could on an average count upon about 46 more years. He would not feel sure of this, of course; only about 386 out of 1,000 males aged ten would be alive 55 years later, when those who thought of retiring from gainful employment might do so. Many preferred not to retire, nor could they be pushed out by union rules, bureaucracy, or ambitious younger employees.

The continuing threat of incapacitating illness was of equal importance to the worker of earlier eras. If a male reached the age of 65 he could on an average count upon about 10 more years. Throughout life, however, he was exposed to illnesses which could greatly reduce his capacity to earn a living. Medicine had not yet attained the curative powers we expect from it today, nor were man's household and workshop environments so well adapted to shielding him against exposure to physical ill and pain. Sustained exposure to an unsalubrious environment left its mark on man even as did recurring illness, much as drought upon the width of a tree's rings.

With life expectancy held low and with the threat of incapacitating illness ever about, man tended to value the present much more highly than the future, especially that future which lay beyond the period of his withdrawal from the labor force. Presumably, the length of life after work would be too short to warrant much planning. As late as 1900, a young man of 20 could expect to live another 42.2 years, of which 39.4 would be spent at work. Moreover, as long as most males lived in rural communities they could find something to do until incapacitation finally forced them to live with or near their children. A century ago nearly 75 percent of the population was nonurban— more than double the percentage so situated today.

Even the present called for little planning. Discretionary income was negligible, as was discretionary time, when the workweek ran 60 hours and more. Man was kept so busy coping with the present that he could do little more than let the future look after itself. Often he could not even meet Ovid's injunction in *Tristia* (III, 4, 25) : "Well doth he live who lives retired and keeps his wants within the limit of his means."

Today, because of the prolongation of education, man does not reach an income-planning period until he is in his twenties. In 1960 male life expectancy at age 20 was 49.6 years, of which 42.6 would be spent at work; by the year 2000, the corresponding figures may be around 54 and 45. The number of years of expected worklife per year of expected retirement fell from 14.1 in 1900 to 6.1 in 1960, and may approximate 5 by 2000. Should male life expectancy at 20—about 50 for whites in 1966—rise to 55, 828 of each 1000 males aged 20 would reach 65, and could then look forward to an average of 15 years more of life. A female of 65 could expect at least 2 or 3 more years of life than a male of that age.

Today's male thus has more nonworking time to allocate than did a male in 1900. Then at age 60 he had about 14 additional years, whereas today he has 16 or more. Today he works 40 hours or less per week, whereas in 1900 he worked about 60. In addition to this discretionary time, he usually has more discretionary income than the generations that preceded him.

It is nevertheless quite possible that allocation, especially with respect to the future, will assume less importance as the years pass. The threat of thermonuclear war is increasing, and with it the probability of death for many tens of millions, as well as the destruction of capital that might be accumulated for future use. Civil disorder is on the increase, with the result that the future becomes less and less attractive. Furthermore, the future may prove to be one of creeping disease. Man's ever more crowded environment is becoming increasingly unhealthy, ridden with pollution and shot through with noise; and his own eating and recreational habits are weakening his bodily resistance to disease. New diseases are emerging to take the place of those partly conquered. "There is as yet no solution in sight," writes René Dubos, for the "new plagues of civilized life."

The allocation of time has many dimensions, as Professor Kreps shows, but two stand out. The first relates to man's entry to gainful activity. Today, if we abstract from nursery school, a young person will spend at least 12 years and very often 16 or 17 years in the educational system. Yet no more than 12 years are actually required to enable a student to complete training of the sort he acquires in these 16–17 years, and no more than nine are needed to complete that ac-

quired in the first twelve years. As a result, the present-day student
foregoes the earnings (of 7 to 10 thousand dollars per year) he would
have enjoyed had he entered the labor force three or four years earlier, and he and the taxpayer bear three or four years more of direct
educational cost beyond what seems necessary. Moreover, the negligible demands made upon youth in our educational system allow him
to develop habits which fit him badly for his later worklife. Society
suffers accordingly. As H. J. Mackinder noted in another connection,
if men's habits are thrown out of gear with one another, society loses
its momentum (its "Going-Concern" character), with the result that
only force remains as a means of restoring discipline. A youth who
enters the labor force three to four years earlier is more likely to acquire the habits requisite to sustaining orderly social momentum.

Consider now the second major dimension of man's allocation of his

Figure 0.1. Work capacity and work requirements of employment over time

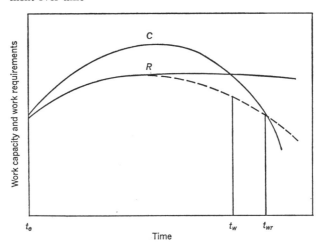

time. This relates to his later years, to the years immediately preceding and succeeding retirement. More specifically, it relates to the disparity between man's physical withdrawal from worklife in his later
years and his prior expulsion from work by society's contemporary institutional restrictions. A distinction needs to be made, therefore, between the physical and mental requirements of employment and man's
capacity to meet these requirements.

For illustrative purposes see Figure 0.1, where time is measured
along the abscissa, and both capacity and requirements along the
ordinate. The curve C traces man's lifetime capacity to meet the re-

quirements of his employment, which is denoted by curve R.[1] It is supposed that at time t_e when man enters the labor force his capacity is roughly equal to the demands made upon it. Thereafter, the curve R rises, usually to a plateau from which in the end it may even descend. The curve C, however, probably rises faster than R, also to a plateau from which it eventually descends. Throughout most of worklife, man's capacity to meet the requirements of his occupation exceeds these requirements; he enjoys a surplus of capacity that is likely to be drawn on only in times of emergency. Later on, of course, the capacity curve bends down and intersects the requirements curve (at t_w) , even if the latter is permitted to turn down somewhat as in Figure 0.1 (at t_{wr}) ; then the time for retirement is at hand unless corrective measures can be taken.

Two kinds of action may shift the point of intersection to the right. First, requirements may be reduced through change in the technological aspects of an occupation. This has been done in respect of the physical demands of employment, most of which have been greatly reduced. Mental requirements have, however, increased in many instances, and so have those constituting what may be called "personal responsibility."

Second, the C curve may be raised for most individuals, especially in its later reaches. The raising process is a long-continued one. It begins at a very early age, since general capacity takes shape very early in childhood, being conditioned by a child's physical-mental environment. It continues while the maturing individual is undergoing formal education and subsequently when he undergoes periodic retraining. It is affected also by his mode of living. For example, it will tend to be greater if his recreation is predominantly participatorial instead of spectatorial, as it is in soporific television-ridden societies.

Turn now to Figure 0.2, which relates not merely (as with Figure 0.1) to the occupational aspect of man's life but rather to the whole of his participation in the life of state and community. Time is measured along the abscissa, and both participation, designated by curve P, and capacity to participate, designated by curve C, are measured along the ordinate. The curves as drawn indicate that actual participation almost always falls below the individual's capacity to participate. The representative individual is assumed to begin to participate at some time t_e before his rate of participation rises to a maximum level at t_f; thereafter he maintains his maximum rate until t_w. At t_w he begins to

1. On the relation of job performance to age, see Juanita M. Kreps, "Job Performance and Job Opportunity: A Note," *Gerontologist,* 7 (March, 1967) , 24–27.

Figure 0.2. Individual lifetime capacity and participation

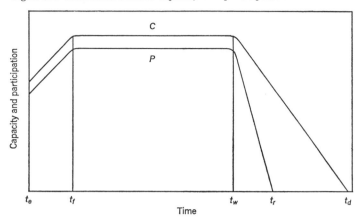

reduce his participation, to withdraw from at least some community activities, to disengage from collective life. Since he is not forced by physical incapacity to withdraw so rapidly from full participation, it may be inferred that he is being forced by conventions, rules, and arbitrary presumptions to withdraw. As the chart is drawn, withdrawal proceeds more rapidly than decline in capacity, becoming complete at t_r although death does not occur until t_d. Under ideal conditions withdrawal would proceed at the same pace as the decline in capacity, with the result that the ratio of degree of participation to capacity to participate would continue to approximate unity. Institutions bearing upon the aged need to be reformed to perpetuate such a relationship.

It should be possible to move C and P into closer proximity. If this is done, the welfare of the aged will be greatly increased. The possibility of such parallel movement is closely connected, however, with how income, work, and time are allocated—a connection made clear by Professor Kreps, especially in her discussions contained in Parts III and IV.

In the preceding comments I have focused attention upon the relative deprivation to which the aged remain subject in an emerging age of luxury and leisure and in what Patten would have called a "pleasure economy," if not yet a "creative economy." It is mainly with the dimensions of a "pleasure economy" that Professor Kreps is concerned. The distribution over a representative individual's lifetime of his time and income, and his expenditure of each are delineated with precision, and proximate prospects are disclosed. American conditions are contrasted with those encountered elsewhere, and ways of eliminating poverty and improving man's lifetime allocation of time and money are examined.

Of necessity, several problems have had to be passed over by the author. As Pareto foresaw, relative poverty cannot be eliminated; yet this factor has not been treated here. After all, human differences are great, and bureaucratic definitions of poverty are elastic upward. Further distinctions need to be made between poverty defined in budgetary terms and poverty defined in subjective terms, particularly since man's welfare is closely correlated with his own image of his role and condition. This distinction would make apparent the degree of illfare caused by the political generation of expectations which are economically unsatisfiable—a condition not yet present early in this century, when expectations were still essentially sequelae to economic improvement.

Ultimately, no issue is of greater long-run concern than the question of *how* man uses his increasing income and discretionary time. Poets have told us that every empire expires in the soft lap of luxury. Gibbon describes how, in a few years, indolence and luxurious living reduced the Vandals, once fierce conquerors of the Romans, to cowardice, ignominy, and self-pity. Manifestations of dissipative processes are already evident in the West. Perhaps the time is at hand when men interested in the preservation of the culture of the West must invent moral equivalents to work and poverty, which are now vanishing from the scene.

I. WORK AND INCOME THROUGH THE LIFESPAN

1. THE TIMING OF WORK AND INCOME

The study of income distribution, a subject of centuries of economic analysis, has in the past been concerned primarily with differences in income levels, or with the determination of functional shares: wages, rent, interest, and profits.[1] These traditional allocation issues have not disappeared from the literature of recent years. However, some of today's urgent questions turn on the division of the national product between persons who are currently at work and persons who are not—the latter including not only the sick and disabled but also the young and the old.

Changes in the nature of the income-distribution discussion are due in part to a certain ambivalence in our economic ideology. On the one hand we tend to rely on the productivity of a man's labor or that of his capital to determine the size of his income; on the other, we recognize that some persons throughout their lives and all persons during some portion of their lives do not receive income from either source. The confrontation of economic ideology with economic reality is taking place under the banner of the guaranteed annual income, one of the most controversial economic issues of the day.

Debate surrounding minimum income proposals has paid surprisingly little heed to the amount and the timing of work as determinants of family income. Yet the timing of work largely dictates the time pattern of income and influences our views on the adequacy of income at different ages; it is but natural, we reason, for youth to be fashionably impoverished and for old age to be only meagerly fi-

1. Most of the material in chaps. 18 and 9, was published in "Aging and Financial Management," in Matilda W. Riley et al., *Aging and Society*, 2 (New York: Russell Sage Foundation, 1969), 201–228.

nanced. A lengthening of both these nonearning periods, which during the twentieth century has resulted in an additional decade of time free of work, now poses a new set of questions regarding the appropriate allocation of work and income through the lifespan.

There is first the question of leisure-goods preference: what is the ideal division of productivity gain, as between goods and time free of work? Are people's preferences being met? Or does the growth in leisure reflect, instead, slow economic growth and inadequate job creation rather than a preference for free time? The second issue has to do with the temporal distribution of free time and its relationship to the receipt of income. As work comes to be concentrated in the middle years, the maintenance of income through the lifespan obviously becomes more difficult. The allocation of more leisure to retirement years, for example, necessitates a different view of the role and magnitude of income transfers. Although low levels of income may be acceptable for short periods of time, they cannot be lightly dismissed when they prevail during as much as two decades at the end of life. Income maintenance in the future is likely to be increasingly concerned with young and old families, and the question of income adequacy for these age groups will persist.

While an individual family may smooth its lifetime income by saving in some stages and dissaving in others, the bulk of the income transfers are now made in the public sector. In this area the shift is primarily from the taxpayer to the beneficiary, and thus to a large extent from one generation to another. The third set of questions hinges on the nature of this public tax-benefit scheme: To what extent do public transfers redistribute income between income classes? Intergenerational transfers will obviously reapportion income from earners to nonearners, the recipients generally being an extremely low-income group. But insofar as the payroll tax is the basis of tax collections, the degree of this redistribution is limited, perhaps to an exchange from middle- to low-income families. Estimates of the redistributional effects of present and proposed income-maintenance arrangements, which have until recently not been attempted, could provide important policy guidelines.

Although many of these questions have been rigorously studied, systematic analysis of the patterns of work, leisure, and income and their allocation through the lifespan is lacking. Nor has there been any attempt to suggest alternative temporal arrangements which might improve the utility of leisure and of income, as well as minimize the problem of income maintenance during certain stages of the life cycle.

In this study, a review of the interrelationships of work and income directs attention first to the growth of free time in the United States and to current attitudes toward the new leisure. Conflicting views as to the value of leisure are quickly evident; strangely soft is the praise of this component of progress. But the faint praise of free time in this country could be explained in part by the form of the leisure; would longer annual vacations, for example, be more often applauded than early retirement? If so, can the drift toward retirement leisure be attributed to scarce job opportunities, and a tendency to reduce the length of worklife, rather than the length of the workyear, because the former appears to industry to be more efficient?

An examination of postwar patterns of work and leisure in several Western European economies reveals a set of leisure preferences somewhat different from our own. Among nations enjoying high growth rates, where labor has been in short supply and leisure at a premium, growth in nonworking time has taken the form of reduced weekly hours on the job, longer vacations, some reduction in the labor force activity of youth; no discernible movement toward early retirement has occurred, however. Apportioning their increases in leisure largely to the working years, these nations have not been faced with the growing retirement-income problem now confronting the United States.

Recent cross-national study has demonstrated an inverse relation between income and work—specifically, between per capita income and the average number of hours worked per year. The United States' short workyear is of course consistent with its high-income position. The scientific and technological progress that has raised productivity and incomes continues to free man of work not only by permitting him to work a small proportion of the hours in a year but also by allowing him to work a smaller proportion of his total lifetime. But the very process of economic growth that insures gradually rising real income for persons at work has the effect of widening the income gap between the workers and those whose income claims are based on previous earnings. Deterioration in the relative position of retirees occurs even when prices are stable, because the growth in income occurs primarily in the form of current wages and profits.

The impact of economic growth on the earnings of workers as they move through worklife, combined with the increases in earnings attributable to the experience and knowledge gained on the job, raises individual incomes throughout the working years. A man's peak income is typically achieved during the decade prior to his retirement; the drop in income at the time of his withdrawal from the labor force is therefore likely to be quite sharp. But even the income received at the beginning of the retirement period gives him a better position vis-à-vis other consumers than he will be able to maintain. For during his fifteen years or so of retirement, earnings of the economically active will continue to rise while his own money income will improve little or none at all.

Tying public retirement benefits to the cost of living would not solve the problem of keeping retirement incomes in line with earnings. Instead, a scheme for relating benefits to the growth in real per capita income would be required, since these benefits are beginning to constitute the bulk of retirees' incomes. Were such a plan invoked, the redistributive impact of public transfers would be much enlarged, particularly if retirement comes to absorb more and more of the leisure available.

The possibility of a further concentration of work, and the related income issues, raise the question of changes in savings consumption patterns during later life. To what extent would a reordering of consumption from age 50 on enable a family to avoid the sharp drop in level of living now experienced at retirement? What would retirement incomes be if the wage or salary increases received after age 50 were accumulated, at interest, for the retirement period? Would such savings, plus a decumulation of assets during retirement, have a significant effect on the level of living after the end of worklife? A simple model indicates the variables affecting the answers to these questions: retirement age, life expectancy, rate of growth in income, size of transfers, etc.

Retirement age is obviously not only a critical variable, but one whose precise dimension is unpredictable. Should the "normal" year of retirement drop from 65 to 62, the volume of individual saving or public transfers necessary to provide a given level of living would of course increase. One analytical approach—that of estimating the income tradeoff involved in adding or subtracting a working year—is indicated, as a device for placing a monetary value on the marginal year of leisure. In realistic terms leisure years may be taken despite the cost, since they are primarily determined by institutional arrangements and aggregate demand, rather than by individual choice.

The two chapters immediately following discuss the role of leisure in the contemporary economic scene, indicating some of the attitudes toward free time, and the problems involved in maintaining incomes during the nonworking years.

2. LEISURE IN A WORK-ORIENTED SOCIETY *

Mr. Creech, it is said, wrote on the margin of the Lucretius which he was translating, "Mem.—When I have finished my book, I must kill myself." And he carried out his resolution. Life . . . is a dreary vista of monotonous toil, at the end of which there is nothing but death, natural if it so happen, but if not, voluntary, without even a preliminary interval of idleness. To live without work is not supposed to enter our conceptions.[1]

The contemporary intellectual revolution, generally referred to by the technical word, automation, is providing machines which . . . assuming drudgery and monotonous repetitive operations, increase productivity. Within the industrial system a relentless logic necessitates abundance. Leisure, as we experience it, becomes a function of an unseen but very real and enormously fruitful configuration of scientific concepts and theories.[2]

Transition from the first of these two views—that the purpose of life being work, life itself might well end when work ends—to the second—that life is greatly enriched by a technology which reduces the amount of work necessary—has not been an orderly one, and even today there is no unanimity of opinion as to the value of leisure.

---

* The discussion in this chapter is drawn from Juanita M. Kreps and Joseph J. Spengler, "The Leisure Component of Economic Growth," *Technology and the Economy: The Employment Impact of Technological Change*, appendix vol. 2, National Commission on Technology, Automation, and Economic Progress, 1966.

1. Leslie Stephen, "Vacations," reprinted from *Cornhill Magazine,* vol. 20 (1869), in Eric A. Larrabee and Rolf Meyersohn, *Mass Leisure* (Glencoe, Ill.: Free Press, 1958), pp. 281–290.

2. Paul F. Douglass, foreword to "Recreation in the Age of Automation," *Annals of the American Academy of Political and Social Science,* 313 (September, 1957), ix.

ATTITUDES TOWARD LEISURE

Twentieth-century views of leisure are often difficult to fathom. In contrast to Aristotle's belief that "the goal of war is peace, of business, leisure," the uneasy feeling that life with little work has little purpose seems to pervade much of today's thought. Contemporary writers often deplore the growing freedom from work, which provides "a great emptiness," devoid of meaning. Lacking training for leisure and having no strong interests or devotions, one author argues, persons without work lead dismal lives. The void created by leisure has thus replaced "the days when unremitting toil was the lot of all but the very few and leisure was still a hopeless yearning." [3] In less extreme form, concern is frequently voiced over the idleness forced upon youth because of lack of job opportunities and on the elderly because of early and compulsory retirement from work.

Americans have traditionally believed, according to Margaret Mead, that leisure should be earned before it is enjoyed. The function of recreation is to prepare man for further work, and as soon as it appears that there will be more time available than is actually needed for this purpose

> alarm spreads over the country. People are going to have too much leisure. . . . This means more time than is needed to relax and get back to work again—unearned time, loose time, time which, without the holding effects of fatigue before and fatigue to come, might result in almost anything. [4]

Unfortunately, experience has indicated that changes in the relationship between time at work and time free for leisure have often resulted in boredom and apathy or excessive and frantic activity. But the philosophy that leisure must be earned and reearned has changed since World War II, the author continues. It is the home and family that now stand center stage, and the job is subsidiary to the good life. Men value jobs that allow them a maximum of time at home and a minimum of strain and overwork on the job. "As once it was wrong to play so hard that it might affect one's work, now it is wrong to work

3. Robert M. MacIver, *The Pursuit of Happiness* (New York: Simon and Schuster, 1955). Chap. 6 is reprinted in Larrabee and Meyersohn, *Mass Leisure*, pp. 118–122.
4. Margaret Mead, "The Pattern of Leisure in Contemporary American Culture," *Annals of the American Academy of Political and Social Science*, 313 (September, 1957), 13.

so hard that it may affect family life."[5] But in contrast, Robert M. MacIver argues that the growing freedom from work merely provides "a great emptiness" for all but the placid people, and the placid are diminishing in number. "The days of unremitting toil" are thus removed, but the change is not necessarily for the better.[6]

How the workers feel about "unremitting toil" or even toil during relatively short workweeks is revealing. Robert Dubin reports that for three out of every four industrial workers he studied, work and the workplace are not central life interests. Although the worker recognizes the primacy of work he does not have a sense of total commitment to it, nor does he view his work or working relationships as the major source of his enjoyment, happiness, or sense of worth. The author suggests that "the problem of creating an industrial civilization is essentially a problem of social invention and creativity in the non-work aspects of life,"[7] as an earlier conference had concluded.[8] These inventions are likely to come, not in connection with worklife, but within the framework of community life.

Our sense of responsibility for how other people spend their leisure time is characteristic of American life; indeed, as David Riesman says, "our bonanzas, our windfalls . . . have been interpreted by the most sensitive and responsible among us as problems."[9] We are proud, in fact, of being such responsible members of society that we ourselves have no leisure. But the author argues that criticism of the work-oriented Puritans is probably overdone. The moral seriousness of puritanism has in fact helped to bring society to the position in which leisure can become a problem for a majority of the people.

The problems inherent in the acquisition and assimilation of leisure are comparable, the author continues, to problems that arise in other areas of social progress; "Every social advance is ambivalent in its consequences." Being at the frontier of the development of leisure, we have of course conflicts in attitudes toward its use. Knowing very little about what leisure means to people—how much they read, for example, or how widespread is the interest in painting or chamber music—we make assumptions that may in fact considerably understate

5. Ibid., p. 14.

6. MacIver, *The Pursuit of Happiness*. Chap. 6 is reproduced in Larrabee and Meyersohn, *Mass Leisure*, pp. 110–122.

7. Robert Dubin, "Industrial Workers' Worlds," *Social Problems,* 3 (1956), 131–142.

8. Eugene A. Staley, ed., *Creating an Industrial Civilization* (New York: Harper, 1952).

9. David Riesman, "Some Observations on Changes in Leisure Attitudes," *Antioch Review,* 12 (1952–1953) 417–436.

the nation's capacity for activities which earlier work schedules have prohibited.

Currently there are a number of areas of pioneering in leisure: music, painting, and literature; sociability and conversation; sports. While these fields are being developed for masses of people, anxieties as to the values of leisure and the merits of using it in particular ways are to be expected. But Mr. Riesman argues that only historical amnesia can blind one to the humanizing effects of reduced work (including the elimination of child labor) and increased time free of work.

The extent of recent changes in attitude toward leisure is of course difficult to estimate, although there is ample evidence, both in the pressure for a statutory reduction in the workweek and in union negotiations for reduced hours per week, longer vacations, earlier retirement, etc., that increased free time is being actively pursued. The critical question whether this pursuit reflects a genuine desire for free time, or whether it is primarily an attempt to increase the number of jobs, appears not to be currently at issue. Instead, labor leaders usually argue that as long as there is unemployment the workweek is too long, and

> aside from the workers' desire for their paid holidays and paid vacations, there is no evidence that workers want shorter daily or weekly hours. The evidence is all on the other side. Hundreds of local and international officials have testified that the most numerous and persistent grievances are disputes over the sharing of overtime work. The issue is not that he has been made to work, but that he has been deprived of a chance to make overtime pay. Workers are eager to increase their income, not to work fewer hours.[10]

The question whether increases in nonworking time are chosen in preference to increased incomes or whether leisure will grow only as a result of efforts to spread the work may turn, in part, on the form of the potential leisure. A reduction in the workweek, for example, may have much less utility to the worker than an increase in vacation time. Leisure in the form of early retirement may have the lowest utility of any form of free time (save unemployment). If free time is to grow

10. George Brooks, "History of Union Efforts to Reduce Working Hours," *Monthly Labor Review,* 79 (November, 1956), 1273. However, see the discussion of the consumers' purchase of leisure, and the increase in leisure through reduced nondiscretionary time, in Justin Voss, "The Definition of Leisure," *Journal of Economic Issues,* 1 (June, 1967), 91–106.

as technology improves—if in fact leisure is to be as characteristic of our times and "as representative of our modern spirit as the Parthenon was an expression of the age of Athens" [11]—the form in which this leisure emerges is of some significance. Not only does the temporal distribution of leisure affect its value, the distribution of income through the life cycle is also influenced by the apportionment of working and nonworking time.

THE GROWTH AND DIMENSIONS OF LEISURE

Today's worker receives the equivalent of a 4-month holiday, paid, each year. If he followed his grandfather's schedule of hours per week, he could work from October through May, then vacation till October. Or if he preferred, he could work April through November, and ski all winter.

He takes his nonworking time in different forms, but in total he enjoys about 1,200 hours per year more free time than did the worker of 1890. Moreover, he enjoys more years in which he doesn't work at all; he enters the labor force much later in life, and has several more years in retirement than his grandfather. In total, this increase at the beginning and the end of worklife has given him about 9 additional nonworking years. Yet lest the worker of today be labeled a loafer, it should be noted that since he lives longer, he works more hours in his lifetime than his predecessor; if born in 1960 he will probably log about 6,800 more hours than the male born in 1900.

On the average, the employed person works about 40.5 hours a week at present; in 1890, the average was 61.9.[12] Paid holidays have in-

11. Douglass, "Recreation in the Age of Automation," p. ix.

12. For historical data on hours of work, vacation time, paid holidays, sick leave, etc., see *Hours of Work*, Hearings before the Select Subcommittee on Labor of the Committee on Education and Labor, House of Representatives, 88th Congress, 1963, Parts I and II, particularly the summary data presented by Ewan Clague, pp. 73–104 of Part I. See also, J. Frederick Dewhurst and Associates, *America's Needs and Resources* (New York: Twentieth Century Fund, 1955), and various *Monthly Labor Review* articles, including: Arnold Strasser, "Plant and Paid Leave Hours in Manufacturing, 1959 and 1962," 88 (April, 1965), 413–415; Frances Jones and Dorothy Smith, "Extent of Vacations with Pay in Industry, 1937," 47 (July, 1938), 269–274; unsigned, "Vacations with Pay in Union Agreements, 1940," 51 (November, 1940), 1070–1077. See also "Paid Sick Leave Provisions in Major Union Contracts, 1959," Bureau of Labor Statistics, *Bulletin Number 1282* (November, 1960); Enzo Puglisi, "Employer Expenditures for Selected Supplementary Remuneration Practices for Production Workers in Manufacturing Industries, 1959," Bureau of Labor Statistics, *Bulletin Number 1308* (January, 1962); and Seymour Wolfbein, "Changing Patterns of Working Life," United States Department of Labor, Manpower Ad-

creased by at least 4 percent during this period, to about 6 at present, and paid vacations averaging 1½ weeks per year have added at least 6 days free time annually. Sick leave amounts to the equivalent of 1 week, giving the increases in nonworking hours per year between 1890 and the present shown in Table 2.1.

Table 2.1. Increases in nonworking hours per year from 1890 to the present

Source	Approximate hours
Reduction in workweek (21.2 hours per week)	1,100
Increase in paid holidays (4 days)	32
Increase in paid vacations (6 days)	48
Increase in paid sick leave (1 week)	40
Total increase	1,220

Thus the shortened workweek has accounted for most of the century's rise in free time during worklife. The addition of 9 years of nonworking time raises the male's number of years outside the labor force by about 50 percent. If, instead of spending this free time in gaining additional education and in retirement, man worked on the average 2,000 hours per year during these years, he would work during his lifetime an additional 18,000 hours, or 435 hours per year (with a worklife expectancy of 41.4 years). Thus the amount of nonworking time bunched at the beginning and end of worklife has grown by about one-third the amount added annually through workweek reductions, added vacations, etc.[13]

ministration (August, 1963). Several articles by Peter Henle deal with the overall growth in leisure; see his "Recent Growth of Paid Leisure for U.S. Workers," *Monthly Labor Review,* vol. 85 (March, 1962), and "The Quiet Revolution in Leisure Time," *Occupational Outlook Quarterly,* 9 (May, 1965), 5–9. An earlier summary by Joseph Zeisel, "Labor Force and Employment in 1959," appeared in *Monthly Labor Review,* vol. 83 (May, 1960). Finally, see Clyde E. Dankert and Associates, *Hours of Work* (New York: Harper, 1965), which is a series of analytical articles by Herbert R. Northrup, Richard L. Rowan, Ray Marshall, W. R. Dymond and George Saunders, Paul E. Mott, Frederic Meyers, Floyd C. Mann, Dean F. Berry, David G. Brown, Clyde E. Dankert, and Melvin W. Reder.

13. The definitions of leisure are many. At one extreme, the term is used to denote all nonworking time; at the other, it applies quite restrictively to that time which is completely free of commitments—contemplative time, in short. The concept of leisure as "discretionary" time has also been developed, and for many purposes this is the most meaningful use of the word leisure. However, it is important at the outset to indicate the dimensions of present and future time free of work done for pay; for the moment, this nonworking time is referred to arbitrarily as leisure.

LEISURE VERSUS INCOME

"In an economic as in a philosophical or poetical sense," wrote George Soule more than a decade ago, "time must now be regarded as the scarcest of all the categories of basic resources." [14] The notion of scarcity of time has also been emphasized by Wilbert E. Moore, who notes that "in the world of commonsense experience the only close rival of money as a pervasive and awkward scarcity is time." [15]

Given the scarcity of time, the demand for leisure can be treated in the same manner as the demand for goods. Faced with the problem of allocating his time between leisure and goods, the individual will continue to work until the "advantages to be reaped by continuing seem no longer to overbalance the disadvantages." [16] In indifference analysis, the worker maximizes his satisfaction with that combination at which the marginal rate of substitution of leisure for wage goods equals the ratio of the price of leisure to the price of wage goods.

But as Moore, Spengler, and others have pointed out, time and money are not necessarily interchangeable; in many instances, groups of people—the unemployed, for example—may not be able to transform time into goods. Time may therefore have little or no value in economic terms, its utility as leisure, when all time is free of work, being zero. The ability to exchange leisure for goods is also limited for a very large proportion of employed persons, whose annual hours of work are institutionally fixed and whose opportunities for moonlighting are practically nonexistent.

American workers' desire for additional goods, despite our present levels of consumption, is alternately applauded and deplored. Industry in this country caters to the taste for variety in style and form, and mechanical and electrical gadgets, household appliances, automobiles, etc., are readily available. As incomes rise, these goods rapidly become a part of the worker's standard of living; today's luxuries are tomorrow's necessities. Ruth Mack demonstrates the high propensity to consume by calculating the income elasticity for various commodities. Using Kuznets's data, she finds that a 1 percent increase in income produces a 0.95 percent increase in consumption of perishables;

14. *Time for Living* (New York: Viking, 1955), p. 99.
15. *Man, Time, and Society* (New York: Wiley, 1963), p. 4.
16. Alfred Marshall, *Principles of Economics*, 9th ed. (New York: Macmillan, 1961), p. 527n. On the economics of time allocation, see G. S. Becker, "A Theory of the Allocation of Time," *Economic Journal*, 75 (September, 1965), 493–517.

for durables a 1 percent rise in income produces a 1.15 percent increase in consumption, and for services the rise is 1.16 percent.[17]

In documenting the high level of consumption, several factors are often cited: the American housewife's demand that her house be as up to date and shining as possible; the social status conferred by the ownership of goods, particularly consumer durables; the rapid rate of innovation and change in models. The tendency for saving to remain a fairly constant percentage of income has been noted by economists,[18] although it has also been suggested that the composition of future consumption may reflect a very rapid expansion in the services sector.[19] One further indication of the desire for goods rather than leisure is the growth in the number and proportion of married women in the labor force.

The push for reduced working time, given these indications that we prefer more goods to more leisure, must be explained on the basis of the workers' assumption that the total amount of work to be done is limited. In periods of unemployment, this work needs to be spread to all job seekers by reducing each worker's share of the total, or by reducing the number who work. Hence, drives for a shorter workweek or early retirement merely belie a "lump-of-labor" notion and provide no basis for judging the worker's preferences as between leisure and goods. If free choice could be exercised, there would probably be some variation in the selected options, in terms of both the amount of work performed and the pattern of its distribution through the workyear and the worklife.

Productivity gains have accrued to mankind in the forms of higher levels of living and greater free time; current questions turn on the preferred proportions of goods and leisure. But the problem of unemployment has obscured the true nature of the choice, with the result that increasing leisure may come to be regarded primarily as a means of reducing labor force size, despite the evidence that such attempts will do little to solve the problem. Viewed in this manner, free time may continue to increase even if its utility (as compared with the utility of additional goods) is low.

17. Ruth Mack, "Trends in American Consumption and the Aspiration to Consume," *American Economic Review*, 46 (May, 1956) , 57.

18. See Simon Kuznets, *National Products since 1869* (New York: National Bureau of Economic Research, 1946) ; James Duesenberry, *Income, Saving, and the Theory of Consumer Behavior* (Cambridge, Mass.: Harvard University Press, 1949) ; and Milton Friedman, *A Theory of the Consumption Function* (Princeton, N.J.: Princeton University Press, 1957).

19. See Mack, "Trends in American Consumption"; also Nelson N. Foote, "Discussion: The Shortening Work Week as a Component of Economic Growth," *American Economic Review*, 46 (May, 1956) , 227.

3. NONEARNING YEARS AND THE ROLE OF TRANSFERS

*My father taught me to work, but not to love it.
I never did like to work and I don't deny it. I'd
rather read, tell stories, crack jokes, talk, laugh—any-
thing but work.*

Abraham Lincoln

The frequent fear of too much leisure may not be warranted; for most people, work is not likely to be the soul-satisfying experience that the "joy-in-work" philosophers have assumed.[1] Work is often tiring, boring, and quite unpleasant. It is no accident that the pressure for shorter working hours (albeit, with no reduction in pay) has come from industrial and commercial workers, who are much less satisfied with their working conditions than the professional.

The significance of the leisure question turns not on whether there is so much time free of work that life loses its focus but instead on the distribution of leisure over the total population, on the forms the free time is to take, on the cost of the leisure in terms of the product fore-gone, and on sources of financial support during the nonworking years. At the outset, it is important to consider two of these issues—the distribution of leisure and sources of income during nonworking periods.

---

1. See the discussion by Harold L. Sheppard, "Implications of Technological Change for Leisure," in Juanita M. Kreps, *Technology, Manpower, and Retirement Policy* (Cleveland: The World Publishing Company, 1966), pp. 175–184.

THE DISTRIBUTION OF LEISURE

It is increasingly evident that the allocation of nonworking time among the different occupational groups in the labor force is extremely uneven; in recent years, some groups have shared only meagerly in this component of economic growth.

Harold L. Wilensky's analysis of the distribution of leisure shows a disproportionate gain in leisure in mining and manufacturing, and (since 1940) in agriculture. By contrast, civil servants and the self-employed have gained little or none. Certain groups of workers (white-collar workers—salesmen, clerks, proprietors, managers, officials, and most professionals) tend to work full time year round, while rural workers, women, nonwhite, young and old workers are part-time or intermittent employees. Even the professional who takes a 4-week vacation is likely to work 2,400 hours (48 weeks at 50 hours per week) per year for 40 years, or 96,000 hours. The year-round, full-time blue-collar worker with 2 weeks of vacation works 2,000 hours (40 per week for 50 weeks) for 47 years, or 94,000 hours. But since the blue-collar worker seldom works full time for the entire year, his nonworking time far exceeds that of the professional.[2]

The author's conclusion that the upper strata have probably lost leisure during the twentieth century is based upon several findings. Among a sample of lawyers, professors, engineers, and the middle mass (clerks, salesmen, craftsmen, foremen, small proprietors, semiprofessionals, technicians, managers, and some operatives, with incomes ranging from $5,000 to $13,000), about half worked 45 hours or more weekly, and a sizable minority worked 60 hours or more. Ten percent held spare-time jobs at the time they were questioned, and a third had been moonlighters at some time in their worklives. One-third of the high-income men ($10,000 or over) logged 55 hours or more, as compared with one-fifth of those men who made $10,000 or less.

The differences in work schedules within strata are even more pronounced, however. One-fifth of all lawyers and one-fourth of the professors have workweeks of fewer than 45 hours; one-half the engineers and the middle mass have such short workweeks. Being self-employed, Jewish, or high income tends to raise the propensity for long hours. Small proprietors have the longest workweeks (50 percent work 55 hours or more), and solo lawyers are second. Men who con-

2. Harold L. Wilensky, "The Uneven Distribution of Leisure," *Social Problems,* 9 (1961–1962), 32–56.

trol their work schedules (particularly those with incomes of $10,000 or more) work long hours more often than men on fixed schedules.[3] Another author's breakdown of the average hours of business executives shows a workweek of 50 hours—43 at the office plus 7 at home; these hours exclude business entertaining at home, travel time to work, and business travel.[4]

Wilensky concludes that man's quantitative gains in leisure have been exaggerated, and the quality of leisure, being more rigid and fragmented, is far from ideal. Persons with leisure today are of occupational and age groups that either are motivated and able to choose leisure over income or are forced into leisure because of inadequate job opportunities. The former cut across class lines, including college-educated engineers and the upper working class; the latter are concentrated in low-income and low-status jobs where "leisure" takes the form of unemployment and involuntary retirement.

INCOME DURING NONEARNING YEARS

The occupational groups on whom the growing leisure is being conferred appear to be those whose work is the least rewarding psychologically. Unfortunately, their work is also the least rewarding financially. Thus when leisure accrues in the form of reduced worklife, as in the case of earlier retirement, the resulting cost of the free time seems to fall very heavily on the workers whose economic status is precarious even during worklife, and whose low retirement incomes reflect their low lifetime earnings.

Many young adults who have not yet entered the labor force on a full-time basis are similarly disadvantaged during periods of extended education. For the most part, these are single persons or couples who are still enrolled in school, and whose major sources of support are direct supplements from parents; part-time work, particularly by the wife, who often is not in school; scholarship aid; and student loans. Income levels are likely to be low for most of this group, with debts frequently accumulating.

Incomes of the Aged

Data on income levels of persons who have reached normal retirement age can be used to illustrate the financial position of the group

3. Ibid., pp. 39–43.
4. A. Heckscher and Sebastian de Grazia, "Problems in Review: Executive Leisure," *Harvard Business Review*, 37 (1959), 6–16, 144–156.

which is largely outside the labor force. Of the males aged 65 and over, only about one-fourth now work, and most of these have part-time employment. This low labor force activity of older men, which causes many incomes to drop sharply at or near age 65, has been partially offset during the past three decades by an expansion in retirement benefits. Nine out of ten of the nation's 19 million older people have retirement protection of some sort—85 percent are eligible for social security, and another 5 percent for civil service or railroad retirement benefits. About 15 percent of the aged draw private pensions. Of those persons reaching age 65 in the mid-sixties, 97 percent were covered by a public retirement program.[5]

The amount of the benefit, however, is frequently far too low to provide even a poverty level income; as a result, about 30 percent of the aged are classified as poor. Another 10 percent, who would have been poor if they had relied on their own incomes, share homes with relatives who are above the poverty line.[6]

In 1967 the median income for families headed by persons aged 65 and over was $3,928, or 46.2 percent of the median of $8,504 for families headed by persons aged 14–64. For aged unrelated individuals the median was $1,480, which was only 40.5 percent of the median ($3,655) for younger single persons. Roughly half the families with aged heads had money incomes below $3,900; one older family in five had less than $2,000. Of the aged individuals living alone or with nonrelatives, half had incomes below $1,500; one in four had $1,000 or less. Moreover, the figures in Table 3.1 indicate that although the incomes of the elderly have risen during the 1960s, the increases have been smaller than those accruing to the younger population. The relative income position of the aged has therefore worsened, particularly since 1962.[7]

Recognizing the shortcomings of a poverty index based on money income alone, various attempts have been made to take account of family size and composition, place of residence, and other relevant factors. Mollie Orshansky's poor and near-poor indexes, now widely used, permit a regrouping of the poor by age, household status, farm

5. Wilbur J. Cohen, "Improving the Status of the Aged," *Social Security Bulletin,* 29 (December, 1966) , 3–8.

6. Mollie Orshansky, "The Poor in City and Suburb, 1964," *Social Security Bulletin,* 29 (December, 1966) , 22–37.

7. Bureau of the Census, as supplied by the Administration on Aging, Department of Health, Education, and Welfare, 1969. For further detail on incomes of the elderly, see the task force report, *Economics of Aging: Toward a Full Share in Abundance,* Special Committee on Aging, United States Senate, March, 1969, pp. 5–34.

Table 3.1. Median incomes of families classified by age of head of family, and percentage increases, 1960 to 1967

	1960	1961	1962	1963	1964	1965	1966	1967
Families								
Head 14–64								
Amount	$5,905	$6,099	$6,336	$6,644	$6,981	$7,413	$7,922	$8,504
Percentage increase	—	3.3	3.9	4.9	5.1	6.2	6.9	7.3
Head 65 and over								
Amount	$2,897	$3,026	$3,204	$3,352	$3,376	$3,514	$3,645	$3,928
Percentage increase	—	4.4	5.9	4.6	0.7	4.1	3.7	7.8
Percentage of 14–64	49.1	49.6	50.6	50.4	48.4	47.4	46.0	46.2
Unrelated individuals								
14–64								
Amount	$2,571	$2,589	$2,644	$2,881	$3,094	$3,344	$3,443	$3,655
Percentage increase	—	0.7	2.1	9.0	7.4	8.1	3.0	6.2
65 and over								
Amount	$1,053	$1,106	$1,248	$1,277	$1,297	$1,378	$1,443	$1,480
Percentage increase	—	5.0	12.8	2.3	1.6	6.2	3.0	2.6
Percentage of 14–64	41.0	42.7	47.2	44.3	41.9	41.2	41.9	40.5

Source: Bureau of the Census, as supplied by the Administration on Aging, Department of Health, Education, and Welfare, 1969.

and nonfarm residence, and color. Based on estimates of living costs
under different circumstances, Orshansky found that the 1967 thresh-
old income levels for aged families and individuals were: poor—
$2,020 for married couples and $1,600 for nonmarried persons; near
poor—$2,690 for married couples and $1,900 for nonmarried persons.
On the basis of these minimum levels, about 44 percent of the aged
were poor in 1967, and another 11 percent were in the near-poor
classification. Moreover, only about one-third of the aged units had
enough income to purchase the "moderate" level of living, which the
Bureau of Labor Statistics estimated cost just under $4,000 for a re-
tired couple and $2,170 for a single person.[8]

The 1968 Survey of the Demographic and Economic Characteristics
of the Aged revealed a median income for aged couples of $3,373, a
median for aged men of $1,692, and a median for aged women of
$1,227 (Table 3.2). Only 3 percent of all aged units had incomes of

Table 3.2. Income size: Percentage distribution of aged units by money income class,
1967

Total money income	All units	Married couples	Nonmarried persons		
			Total	Men	Women
Number (in thousands)					
Total	15,779	5,989	9,789	2,356	7,434
Reporting on income	12,186	4,417	7,770	1,954	5,816
Percentage of units	100	100	100	100	100
Less than $1,000	21	3	31	20	36
1,000–1,499	19	6	26	23	27
1,500–1,999	14	11	16	18	15
2,000–2,499	10	12	10	15	8
2,500–2,999	7	11	5	7	4
3,000–3,499	6	10	3	4	3
3,500–3,999	4	9	2	3	1
4,000–4,999	6	11	3	4	2
5,000–7,499	7	15	2	3	2
7,500–9,999	3	7	1	2	1
10,000–14,999	2	3	1	1	1
15,000 or more	1	2	1	1	1
Median income	$ 1,828	$3,373	$1,306	$1,692	$1,227

Source: Social Security Bulletin, 33 (April, 1970), 8.

8. Leonore E. Bixby, "Income of People Aged 65 and Older: Overview from 1968
Survey of the Aged," *Social Security Bulletin*, 33 (April, 1970), 3–34; Bureau of
Labor Statistics, "Retired Couple's Budget for a Moderate Living Standard," *Bulletin Number 1570–4* (1968) ; and Mary H. Hawes, "Measuring Retired Couples' Living Costs in Urban Areas," *Monthly Labor Review*, 92 (November, 1969) , 3–16.

$10,000 or more. Almost half (46 percent) of the aggregate income of the elderly came from retirement benefits, while 29 percent came from earnings and 15 percent from assets.[9]

The relative importance of these components of income varied with the size of the income (Figure 3.1). For those units with high levels of

Figure 3.1. Sources of income of aged units by size of income, 1967

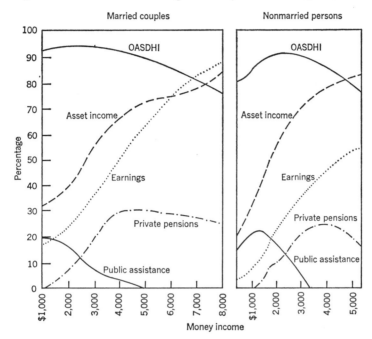

Source: Social Security Bulletin, 33 (April, 1970), 17.

income, earnings and asset income were significant. But whereas Old Age and Survivors Disability Health Insurance (OASDHI) benefits accrued to nine out of ten of the aged, these benefits were relatively less important to the older unit whose income was high, and relatively more important to the low- and moderate-income retiree. For the very low levels, public assistance (which averaged only $70 a month) was important, being combined in half the assistance cases with low OASDHI benefits. Asset income, which is directly correlated with size

9. Bixby, "Income of People Aged 65 and Older," p. 8.

of income, was reported far more often for elderly couples than for older single persons.[10]

TRANSFER PAYMENTS DURING RETIREMENT

The sources of the elderly's income have shifted markedly during the past twenty years, with earnings coming to be a smaller, and income-maintenance programs a much larger, proportion of the total. About 46 percent of their aggregate income in 1967 came from social insurance, other public pensions, and private group pensions. Veterans' benefits and public assistance added another 7 percent of the total. Earnings accounted for 29 percent and income from assets another 15 percent of the total. Cash contributions by friends or relatives not living in the same household amounted to 1 percent of the total income.[11]

The growing significance of income maintenance to the support of the aged underscores the need for frequent scrutiny of the role of public transfer payments: their adequacy (however defined), the tax source, possible rates of growth in benefits, etc. Currently, public officials are reexamining the question of income supplements for all low-income groups. If a guaranteed income plan is adopted, aggregate transfers will of course be much larger, and it will be necessary to depart from the present scheme of payroll taxes, which provide the funds for most of the aged's claims. Payroll-tax financing will probably give way to a partial general-revenue scheme in any case, because of repeated criticisms of the payroll tax's regressivity.

Under the present arrangement, financed by payroll taxes on the incomes of persons at work and their employers, income claims against the nation's total output are transferred from persons at work and consumers in general (assuming that the employer's share of the tax is shifted to the consumer in the form of a higher price) to retirees. Ob-

10. Ibid., p. 17. For a broad view of age-related differences in net worth, and the problems of measuring income and net worth, see Burton A. Weisbrod and W. Lee Hansen, "An Income–Net Worth Approach to Measuring Economic Welfare," *American Economic Review*, 58 (December, 1968), 1315–1329; and Dorothy S. Projector and Gertrude E. Weiss, "Income–Net Worth Measures of Economic Welfare," *Social Security Bulletin*, 32 (November, 1969), 14–17.

11. Bixby, "Income of People Aged 65 and Older," p. 11, table 3. Estimates of the aggregate income of the aged taking into account data from additional sources (Internal Revenue Service and administrative records) show a larger percentage coming from assets (25 percent), about the same from earnings (30 percent), and smaller proportions from retirement benefits (37 percent), veterans' benefits, and public assistance (6 percent). Ibid., p. 14.

viously, the transfer is from workers in 1970 to retirees in 1970, and not from a man who works in 1970 to the same man when he retires in 1990. The retiree of 1990 will have an income claim against the 1990 output, and his claim will be financed by a tax on the workers of that year. Transfers thus reallocate the annual output between workers and nonworkers (including the young, the unemployed, the disabled, etc., as well as the old), the measure of this redistribution being dictated by congressional decision.

Public policy in the United States has provided for a floor of income for retirees, but there has not yet been an attempt to use Social Security benefits as a means of smoothing the humps and valleys of income in any broad, life-range manner. The problem of poor fit between earnings and consumption needs persists and is in fact accentuated by the rise in productivity and real earnings of persons at work. A shortening of worklife relative to total lifespan further complicates the problem of financial planning.

Reluctance to provide more generous public pensions for retirees reflects in part a failure to recognize the lengthening retirement period as a new life stage and in part a belief that each family is in charge of its own financial destiny. Hence, private savings are expected to achieve whatever income smoothing, beyond certain minimum pensions, is desired. The difficulty of achieving any significant degree of smoothing through private pensions, however, cannot be overlooked. Alternative solutions to the problem are discussed in chapter 12.

QUERY: A RATIONALE FOR TRANSFERS?

In classical wage theory, earnings are derived from the worker's productivity; under competitive conditions, the wage rate tends to approach the value of the marginal product. Payment of wages below the marginal product cannot persist, since competition for workers will drive up the wage; conversely, attempts to hold wages above the value of the marginal product result in unemployment, rather than higher real wages.

Despite widespread criticism, the notion that real wages are a function of productivity continues to hold sway. Union negotiators base their claims for wage increases on the fact that their productivity is rising, and public officials argue that inflationary pressures can be contained only if the rise in wage rates is limited to the rise in productivity. Although the question of whose productivity is to serve as the basis for wage increases is often vague, there is a clear implication that real wages are dependent on current productivity.

Such a rationale for transfers of income is of course lacking, since no service is rendered during the period of the transfer, if at all. Income claims originate from a variety of circumstances: unemployment, after previous work has provided entitlement; retirement, again after service in covered employment; disability; inability to earn because of old age or youth, etc. There is a common element in all instances, however: each recipient, for one reason or another, is either unable or is severely restricted in his ability to work for pay. The 1967 amendment to the Social Security Act requiring mothers of dependent children to work or enter job training is further evidence of our belief that income claims should accrue only to persons who cannot acquire earnings.

The growing importance of transfers, particularly during youth and old age, calls for a reexamination of this rationale. The inability to work for pay has become an extremely complex matter, involving institutional barriers to employment, as in compulsory retirement cases, levels of aspiration and estimates of the costs and returns from higher education, rates of time preference for goods, leisure-versus-goods preferences, etc.

Even more significant are the lengthening periods of man's life in which his income is determined by the level of transfers. As long as the basis for a transfer is the need to provide short-run financial support until work can be resumed, the tendency is to make the payment minimal; it is, after all, a temporary expedient. But when the period stretches to two decades at the end of life, and in many instances to as much as two and a half decades prior to labor force entry, the nonearning years assume a different dimension. The question then emerges: On what basis is the income level during the nonworking years to be determined? Labor productivity, albeit an imperfect basis for determining earnings even during worklife, ceases to be an index of a man's "worth" when he ceases to work. Nor is the amount of financial support given a student necessarily related to his anticipated worklife productivity.

The theory of income distribution that is couched in marginal productivity terms has never been altogether satisfactory. It is less so when a large portion of one's lifetime income takes the form of an income claim against a current output which he did not help to produce; or conversely, when the workers' output is shared with the nonworking members of society. In a public transfer, the income spreading is horizontal in nature; taxes reduce net incomes of work-

ers, transferring income claims against the current output to nonworkers. A private transfer, too, reapportions the annual product
between wages and transfers. But the receipt of a private pension has
a vertical dimension as well: the recipient has acquired the claim because in some previous period he has presumably foregone a portion
of his earnings (in addition to that taxed away for public pensions),
with the understanding that he would later be reimbursed, with interest. The public retirement transfer is essentially one from a generation of workers to a generation of retirees, whereas the private pension
is a transfer from a generation of workers to a particular group of retirees. The total product may of course be larger because of the
previous saving of the private pensioner, who used his current earnings to further capital accumulation rather than to finance his current
consumption.

In summary, income distribution analysis in its modern context is
complicated by the time dimension—the fact that much of lifetime
income is not received in the period when the work is actually performed—and by the issue of public versus private transfers, which influence the size of the income claims of certain groups vis-à-vis all
other consumers. For policy considerations, some rationale for the
size and source of income transfers would be of immense value in
delineating certain questions: To what extent does the present temporal distribution of income approach the desired distribution? If
reallocation is indicated, what is the role of public, and that of private, transfers? Can we identify certain groups—educational, occupational, geographic—who are poor at certain ages but not at others?
The more pressing questions of income allocation seem today to be
found in the contrasts between the status of the working and that of
the nonworking male (whose labor force status is primarily a function of age), rather than in the traditional study of functional shares.

II. WORKING TIME IN SELECTED COUNTRIES

4. DIFFERENCES IN LABOR FORCE ACTIVITY *

THE QUESTION OF EARLY RETIREMENT

The drift toward early retirement in the United States poses questions of both immediate and long-run significance. Currently, concern arises from the fact that benefit levels of early retirees are usually much lower than those paid to men who retire at age 65 or later. Midway through the 1960s for example, the average monthly benefit paid to men retiring before 65 was about $75, as compared with an average of approximately $105 for males who retired at 65 years or later. Even the full benefit is inadequate when it is the only source of income; clearly retirees cannot be expected to live on the reduced pension. The Advisory Council on Social Security has pointed out that as a result many older persons will have to seek Old Age Assistance. Such a development would in the long run reverse the gradually declining role played by Old Age Assistance, adding to the assistance rolls OASDHI beneficiaries who, according to our earlier expectations, were to acquire adequate retirement pensions.

Social policy thus needs to be reexamined in the light of current practice. Demographic developments of the 1950s and 1960s—in particular, the swell in labor force size occasioned by the entrance of large numbers of young workers—clearly have led to some attempts to drain off labor at the other end of worklife. New technologies have reduced the labor requirements per unit of output, making it possible to reduce working time further still. The rate of economic growth necessary to maintain full employment, given those demographic and tech-

* The material contained in this and the two succeeding chapters is taken from Juanita M. Kreps, *Lifetime Allocation of Work and Leisure*, Social Security Administration Research Report number 22, 1968.

nological conditions, has been inadequate. The impact of the resulting unemployment has been on those workers who suffer some disadvantage in the labor market: the nonwhite, the inexperienced, the poorly educated, the older worker. In the case of many workers in the 62–64 age group, reclassification from an unemployed to a retired status provides a welcome source of support, but it also commits the early retiree to a reduced pension throughout his lengthened retirement period.

If slow growth and unemployment, rather than a desire for increased leisure in old age, are the primary explanations for early retirement, it follows that a tightening of the labor market would tend to draw early retirees back into jobs, assuming no institutional restraints. Moreover, it implies that in fully employed economies with no pressures for early withdrawal from the labor force, workers generally continue to work at least until pensionable age. Finally, one could hypothesize that given the freedom to choose the form in which leisure is taken, workers would choose a pattern of a more even distribution of leisure and work throughout the lifespan, rather than a shortening of potential worklife.

The advantages of the former pattern and the historical trend in this direction were discussed by Clarence Long over a decade ago.[1] During this century a decline in the labor participation rate for men has been offset by a rise in that for women, with the result that the combined rate for 1965 (56.7) was roughly the same as the 1900 proportion (53.7). These overall trends conceal important changes in labor force activity of older men, however. Among males aged 65 and over the rate has fallen from 68.3 in 1890 to 27.6 in 1966; for males aged 60–64 the rate is now down to 79.2 (in contrast to the 95.8 for males aged 45–54).

One research approach which is indicated is an evaluation of the effects on retirement of diverse pressures in the United States: on the one hand, increased job demands arising from current military expenditures and, on the other, inducements to early retirement offered by contractual agreements, as in the automobile industry. Unemployment remains high in some areas, and for some time there may be enough slack in the labor market to make it difficult for older displaced workers to find new jobs.

Through another avenue of research, one may gain insight into workers' preferences as to the amount of leisure and its apportionment among the various forms—shorter hours, longer holidays, post-

1. Clarence D. Long, *The Labor Force under Changing Income and Employment* (Princeton, N.J.: Princeton University Press, 1958), pp. 24–25.

poncd entry into and early retirement from the labor force—by studying the patterns which have emerged in Western European countries during the postwar period. These countries have been characterized by high rates of growth and extremely low levels of unemployment; in fact, scarce labor persists as one of their major problems. Insofar as leisure time has grown, therefore, the growth is likely to reflect a genuine preference for free time rather than a desire for more goods and services.

The allocation of any increase in free time in such an environment is of considerable interest for policy in the United States. Given such freedom of choice as full employment conditions confer, do workers choose to take additional free time by keeping young people in school longer or retiring older workers sooner than previously? Or do they prefer to have their leisure apportioned over the worklife span, with longer holidays and shorter working hours? To the extent that they choose to shorten the worklife span, it becomes necessary to reexamine income maintenance policies.

INTERNATIONAL COMPARISONS OF LABOR FORCE ACTIVITY

Interpretation of the relative values placed on income, work, and leisure requires country-by-country data on labor force activity by age and sex and, in addition, annual hours of work and earnings. Important sources of data are the United Nations, especially the International Labour Office, and other international organizations such as the European Economic Community and the Organization for Economic Cooperation and Development.

Activity Rates and Economic Development

From censuses taken mainly in the years 1950 and 1951, a recent United Nations study compared crude activity rates (percentages of the total population that are economically active) for 107 population groups in 99 geographical areas. Significant differences in definitions and coverage call for caution in interpreting the data, but the study is nevertheless the most detailed analysis available, and the number of countries included is far greater than is usually attempted in cross-national studies.

Regional rates for men and women. European countries, which were fairly homogeneous in stage of economic development, in cultural heritage, and in current demographic pattern, varied little in the proportions of their males who were economically active; the crude activity rates for men in 29 of the 31 areas in Europe fell in the 60 to 69 percent range. In North America the rates generally fell between 55 and 59 percent, as did typical rates in Middle and South America, despite the fact that the latter countries have smaller proportions of their populations in the active age groups. For women, the proportions active ranged from 10 to 40 percent in Europe and from 15 to 24 percent in North America. In Middle and South American countries two-thirds of the reported rates for women fell below 20 percent.

Rates by stage of industrialization. Classification of 72 of the countries into three groups—industrialized, semi-industrialized, and agricultural—revealed a consistent relationship between male activity rates and the degree of industrialization.[2] No clear relation obtained between the crude activity rates for females and the degree of industrialization, however. When male activity rates were standardized to remove the effects of differences among countries in age structure of the population,[3] the average rates were lowest for the industrialized countries, highest for the agricultural countries (Table 4.1).

Trends in industrialized countries. Among the industrialized countries, whose current participation rates for males are the lowest, the trend indicates continued reduction. For ten of the countries which have decennial census data since 1910, the average rate for males 15 and over fell from a 1920 rate of 91 percent to a 1950 level of 86 percent. The extent to which these declines have been concentrated in particular age groups is discussed in the section following. For women, the twentieth-century trend has not been consistent. In

2. The index of industrialization was the proportion of the economically active males engaged in agriculture and related activities. "Agricultural" countries were those having 60 percent or more of the active males engaged in agriculture and related activities; "semi-industrialized" countries, 35 to 59 percent; and "industrialized" countries, less than 35 per cent. The 72 countries included in the classification were those for which adequate data on agricultural employment were available. United Nations, *Sex and Age Patterns of Participation in Economic Activities*, Report 1 of *Demographic Aspects of Manpower* (New York: United Nations, Department of Economic and Social Affairs, 1962), p. 6 and table A-14, which lists the countries in each group.

3. The major determinant of the crude activity rate is the age structure of the population; the higher the proportion of persons of working age, the higher the crude activity rate. To calculate the age-standardized activity rages, the age-specific activity rates in each country were applied to the population in the corresponding age groups of a standard population (in this case, the male population of the Netherlands at the 1947 census). The standardized activity rate for males is the sum of these products, divided by the total number of persons in the standard population. Ibid., p. 13.

Table 4.1. Average activity rates for males for countries classified according to
degree of industrialization, recent population censuses

Degree of industrialization	Unadjusted	Standardized for age structure [a]
Industrialized countries [b]	62.2	60.5
Semi-industrialized countries [c]	57.8	62.8
Agricultural countries [d]	55.2	65.1

[a] The age distribution of men in the Netherlands at the 1947 census was taken as the standard.

[b] Twenty-one countries having less than 35 percent of active males engaged in agriculture and related activities.

[c] Thirty countries having 35 to 59 percent of the active males engaged in agriculture and related activities.

[d] Twenty-one countries having 60 percent or more of the active males engaged in agriculture and related activities.

Source: United Nations, *Sex and Age Patterns of Participation in Economic Activities*, Report 1 of *Demographic Aspects of Manpower* (New York: United Nations, Department of Economic and Social Affairs, 1962), table 3.4. Figures are unweighted means.

the United States and Canada the percentages of women in the labor force increased each decade, and the standardized rates for women rose in Australia, England and Wales, New Zealand, and (very slightly) in the Netherlands. But France, Sweden, and Switzerland show long-term downward trends even when the rates are standardized for age composition. It is difficult to predict the effect of industrialization on the labor force activity of women in the underdeveloped countries, but the majority view seems to hold that the female rate will rise, particularly among young women.

Activity Rates and Age

Variations in overall rates of male labor force activity through time or concurrently from one country to another are due primarily to differences in the proportions of young and older men in the labor force. Among these two groups the variations are quite wide.

Age-specific rates by region. On the average, approximately one-fifth of the boys in the 10–14 age group are economically active in South America and among the indigenous populations of Africa; about three-fourths of the 15–19-year-olds are active in all regions except Asia, which has two-thirds, and North America, which has less than three-fifths. At the other end of the worklife span the differences are also quite marked. In North America and Oceania, on the average 39 percent of the males aged 65 and over remain active; in Europe the average proportion is 44 percent, in Asia and among the nonindigenous populations of Africa 58 percent, in Middle America 68 percent, and in South America 71 percent.

Age-specific rates by stage of industrialization. Sharp differences appear in the labor force rates for boys and elderly men when countries are grouped by stage of industrialization (Table 4.2). In agricultural countries the proportion in the 10–14 age group who are active is about six times the proportion at work in the industrialized countries, and the proportion of men aged 65 and over who are active is almost twice the proportion in the industrialized countries. On the latter point, it is interesting to note that the current average participation rates for elderly men in agricultural countries is approxi-

Table 4.2. Average age-specific activity rates for males in countries classified according to degree industrialization, recent population censuses

Degree of industrialization [a]	Age in years							
	10–14 [b]	15–19	20–24	25–34	35–44	45–54	55–64	65 and over
Industrialized countries	4.1	72.4	91.5	96.7	97.6	95.9	85.6	37.7
Semi-industrialized countries	13.2	70.3	91.8	96.2	97.1	95.9	88.9	61.0
Agricultural countries	23.9	78.4	92.1	96.3	97.5	96.3	91.6	70.1

[a] For basis of classification, see Table 4.1.

[b] Excluding countries where a minimum age limit of 15 years was adopted for enumeration of tl economically active population. There were 3 such cases among the industrialized countries, 2 amor the semi-industrialized, and 3 among the agricultural.

Source: United Nations, *Sex and Age Patterns of Participation in Economic Activities*, table 3.2.

mately the same as the United States' rate at the end of the last century.

Age-specific rates in industrialized countries. Male age-specific rates, averaged for groups of countries, fail to reveal differences between individual countries within the broad categories used. It is important to note the variations, particularly in the utilization of young and older men, in countries that are developed and in many instances making critical decisions on the amount of leisure that can be accommodated and on the apportionment of this leisure.

Disregarding the activity rates for youths aged 10–14 (which show, incidentally, that one-third of Italian males in this age group are labor force participants), the largest proportions of working youth are found in Austria, Denmark, Germany, Italy, and England. Substantially lower rates apply for the Netherlands, Norway, Sweden, and Switzerland and still lower rates for Belgium, France, and Canada.

The United States' rate, by far the lowest, is only slightly more than half that of Austria, Germany, or England (Table 4.3).

At the other end of the worklife span a different pattern appears. For the most part, countries with quite high activity rates for young men have relatively low rates for men aged 65 and over. With the exception of Belgium, the lowest activity rates for older men are found in Austria (which has the highest rate for youth), Germany (whose youth rate is second highest), and England (which has the third lowest rate for older men and the fourth highest rate for young men). The United States, whose rate for youth is the lowest, has a higher participation rate for older men than most other countries; in fact, its rate is substantially exceeded only by that of Switzerland.

Detailed analysis of worklife patterns in various countries will be possible only when more reliable data are available, particularly on work activity of the young and on the extent of part-time employment, and when standardized definitions of participation are used in the collection of data. Finer age breakdowns are also necessary in order to establish age of entry into and retirement from the labor force. Subject to the limitations of the available data, however, one may conclude tentatively that among industrialized countries there is some tradeoff between working time in youth and working time in old age. To the extent that this conclusion is borne out by further study, it suggests that income maintenance may be as much a problem of timing as it is one of total expenditure.

Industrialization and the Length of Worklife

The length of the male worklife also varies somewhat, along with the timing of the economically active period. Analysis of net years of working life in countries classified according to degree of industrialization indicated that the proportion of life spent in the labor force as well as the amount of labor force activity, declines with industrialization.

Worklife by stage of industrialization. Among 37 countries that were classified according to degree of industrialization, the average proportion of lifetime spent in the labor force was 65 percent in the semi-industrialized countries and 70 percent in the agricultural countries. The average number of years of active and inactive life for men varies widely, as shown in Table 4.4.

At birth the male in the industrialized country has eight more years of worklife expectancy than the male in an agricultural country, and he can also expect his nonworking period to be eight years longer. In

Table 4.3. Age-specific activity rates for men in selected countries, recent population censuses

Country [a]	Year	10–14	15–19	20–24	25–34	35–44	45–54	55–64	65 and over
Europe									
Austria	1951	*9.0* [b]	*85.5*	*94.0*	*97.0*	*97.8*	*93.9*	*78.4*	*31.3*
Belgium	1947	5.5 [b]	66.8	82.2	95.8	95.9	91.9	78.4	24.7
Denmark [c]	1950	7.8 [d]	84.2	92.0	97.3	98.4	97.3	90.6	35.9
France [e]	1954	0.8 [d]	59.4	90.4	96.8	97.0	95.3	78.7	36.1
Federal Republic									
of Germany [f]	1950	5.3 [b]	84.7	93.4	95.2	97.2	95.2	80.7	26.8
Italy	1951	*32.2*	*82.0*	*91.5*	*96.5*	*97.6*	*95.2*	*80.3*	*43.7*
Netherlands [g]	1947	7.2 [d]	72.3	92.2	97.5	98.2	97.0	85.0	35.5
Norway	1950	— [h]	73.1	89.8	96.4	98.4	97.6	93.0	42.1
Sweden	1950	1.2 [b]	74.4	90.0	97.1	98.1	96.3	86.6	36.1
Switzerland	1950	1.1 [d]	73.8	90.8	97.2	98.6	97.7	91.7	50.7
England and Wales	1951	— [h]	83.7	94.9	97.9	98.6	97.8	91.5	30.7
North America									
Canada	1951	1.4 [d]	58.5	92.4	96.4	96.7	94.5	85.7	38.6
United States [i]	1950	2.5 [d]	44.6	81.9	92.1	94.5	92.0	83.4	41.5

[a] Classified as industrialized (having less than 35 percent of active men engaged in agriculture and related activities) except Italy, which was classified as semi-industrialized (having 35 to 59 percent of active men engaged in agriculture and related activities).

[b] Data on economically active persons under age 15, tabulated without subdivision, were related to the population aged 10–14 to obtain activity rates. The number of active persons under age 15 was partially estimated since census tabulations showed "under 14 years."

[c] Excludes Faeroe Islands.

[d] Tabulation of the economically active population was confined to persons aged 14 and over. In computing the activity rates, active persons aged 14 were related to the population aged 10–14.

[e] Based on a 5 percent sample of census returns.

[f] Excludes West Berlin and the Saar.

[g] The economically active population includes inmates of prisons and internment camps.

[h] Economic activity of persons under age 15 was not investigated.

[i] Based on a 20 percent sample of census returns.

Note: Figures in italics represent percentages obtained by interpolation of figures for different age groups.
Source: United Nations, Sex and Age Patterns of Participation in Economic Activities, table A-2.

Table 4.4. Average number of years of active and inactive life for men, classified by degree of industrialization

	At birth		At 15 years of age	
Degree of industrialization	Number of active years	Number of inactive years	Number of active years	Number of inactive years
Industrialized countries	42.2	22.8	45.3	9.2
Semi-industrialized countries	35.6	17.2	43.1	6.4
Agricultural countries	33.9	14.4	41.5	4.6

Source: United Nations, *Sex and Age Patterns of Participation in Economic Activities.* Figures are unweighted means.

years of nonparticipation, he thus has about 50 percent more leisure than the man living in an agricultural nation.

Worklife in industrialized countries. Among the advanced countries, which have both longer worklife expectancy and inactive-life expectancy, there is some variation in the number of years spent at work, and the proportion of life expectancy that those years constitute (Table 4.5). Active life as a proportion of life expectancy in the se-

Table 4.5. Expectation of life and average net years of active life for men at birth in selected industrialized countries

		Net years of active life		
Country	Year [a]	Average number	Percentage of expectation of life	Average net years of inactive life
Europe				
Austria	1951	40.5	65.4	21.4
Belgium	1947	37.7	60.8	24.3
Denmark	1950	45.0	66.4	22.8
France	1954	41.8	63.0	24.5
Federal Republic of Germany	1950	41.1	63.6	23.5
Netherlands	1947	44.8	64.6	24.6
Norway	1950	45.4	65.6	23.8
Sweden	1950	44.6	64.6	24.4
Switzerland	1950	45.0	67.8	21.4
England and Wales	1951	44.1	67.0	21.7
North America				
Canada	1951	42.0	63.3	24.3
United States	1950	39.7	60.6	25.8

[a] Year to which the data on economic activity relate.
Source: United Nations, *Sex and Age Patterns of Participation in Economic Activities,* table A-8.

lected countries varies by 7 percentage points. In the United States
the male works only 61 percent, whereas in Switzerland he works 68
percent (and in England 67 percent) of his life. At birth, a male in the
United States has a worklife expectancy which may be as much as
five and a half years shorter than that of a male in a Western European nation, and he will be inactive for as much as four and a half
years longer than some of his European counterparts. Although precise measurement of worklife is not possible, there is nevertheless
sufficient evidence to demonstrate an inverse relation between the
proportion of life spent at work and the level of industrial development.[4]

In many instances there are potentially many more hours of work
than are in actual use. The number of hours worked per year may be
affected, for example, when capital or land is so scarce as to place
limits on total working time. Moreover, when work cannot be pro-
grammed with sufficient skill, and varies seasonally, the length of the
workyear may be considerably shorter than the customary 2,000 to
2,500 hours derived from a 50-week span of 40–50-hour workweeks.[5]

Other factors in worklife. The problem of economic support during
the nonworking period is intimately bound up with the question of
the length of this period and its timing, i.e., whether it comes at the
beginning or at the end of worklife. An equally important question
has been raised by Stuart Garfinkle. In appraising social and economic developments in various countries, he stresses the fact that the
ratio of productive to total population is but one factor to be
considered; what is needed is an index of man-years of productive
capacity that combines the length of worklife with "a measure of the
more intensive training of our work force, and/or with a measure of
the increasing output per man-year." [6] Growth in productivity may
indeed have such profound effects on total output as to bring about
significant changes in the patterns of worklife.

4. See John D. Durand, "Population Structure as a Factor in Manpower and
Dependency Problems of Under-developed Countries," *Population Bulletin of the
United Nations,* no. 3 (October, 1953) , p. 11.
5. Colin Clark and Margaret Haswell, *The Economics of Subsistence Agriculture*
(London: Macmillan, 1964) , pp. 113–114, 121–123, 126, 128, 131, 135–148; Theo-
dore W. Schultz, *Transforming Traditional Agriculture* (New Haven: Yale Univer-
sity Press, 1964) , chap. 4; Juanita M. Kreps and Joseph J. Spengler, "The Leisure
Component of Economic Growth," in *The Employment Impact of Technological
Change,* appendix vol. 2 of *Technology and the American Economy,* Report of the
National Commission on Technology, Automation, and Economic Progress (Wash-
ington: Government Printing Office, 1966) , pp. 388–389.
6. *The Lengthening of Working Life and Its Implications,* United Nations World
Population Conference (New York: United Nations, 1965) , p. 6.

Description of work-leisure patterns in the different countries requires data on length of the workyear as well as length of worklife. Workyear figures (at least as difficult to obtain as activity rates by age and sex) are drawn from information on the workweek, annual and public holidays. In the following chapter the available data are reviewed for selected countries, and the workyear is estimated for 1950 and for 1960 or a later year, in order to see whether working patterns in these countries have been changing during the period following World War II.

5. WORKLIFE AND WORKYEAR COMPARISONS

In order to examine work and leisure patterns in more detail, the study of labor force activity rates, weekly hours, and vacation and holiday time has been limited to five countries—the United States, the United Kingdom, the Federal Republic of Germany, Sweden, and Switzerland. The four European countries typify the highly prosperous nations of postwar Europe, having economic growth rates higher than that of the United States and, with the exception of Switzerland, well-developed social security schemes. In these four countries there are shortages of labor; Germany and Switzerland, especially, have found it necessary to import laborers from Southern Europe in order to meet industry's needs. Unemployment has been negligible, and retraining programs have aimed at serving tight labor markets. In brief, the shortage of laborers has led to the development of various policies that offer incentives to work longer, whereas the American economic climate has been the opposite.

WORKLIFE COMPARISONS

As noted in the preceding chapter, the fraction of life spent in the labor force decreases with increased industrialization and also varies somewhat among advanced countries, considered individually. Table 5.1 shows the variations in number of inactive years and ratio of active years to years of total life expectancy for the five selected countries at mid-century, ranked by years of male economic activity.

The 1950 census data also revealed differences in the timing of work within the lifespan. Of the five study countries, the United States had by far the smallest proportion of young men in the labor

Table 5.1. Years of male economic activity, and proportion of life active at mid-century, various countries

Country	Active years	Inactive years	Proportion of life active
United States	39.7	25.8	60.6
Federal Republic of Germany	41.1	23.5	63.6
England and Wales	44.1	21.7	67.0
Sweden	44.6	24.4	64.6
Switzerland	45.0	21.4	67.8

force; Switzerland, Sweden, England and Wales, and Germany had much higher rates for youth. With the exception of Switzerland, which had a high proportion of its elderly as well as its youth at work, the order was pretty well reversed in the activity rates for men aged 65 and over: Germany had the lowest rate, followed by England and Wales, then Sweden, and the United States (Table 4.3).

Changes in Activity Rates since 1950

A comparison of the 1950 activity rates with the most nearly comparable rates for 1960 or later reveals significant changes in most of the countries (Table 5.2). The problem of intercountry comparability of labor force data, however, discourages any firm conclusions, and changes within the countries over time present even more serious difficulties.

For young men, the decline in labor force activity appeared to be particularly great in Sweden, where the proportion of 15–19-year-olds dropped by more than a third between 1950 and 1965. In the United States 14–19-year-olds had a decline of almost a fifth in roughly the same period, followed by the United Kingdom, Germany (in a shorter period), and Switzerland.

For young women the rates also decreased, though less rapidly; in Sweden from 1950 to 1965, by almost a third; in the United States by a tenth, followed by Germany and the United Kingdom, with the Swiss proportion remaining the same. For both sexes, the proportions of youth in the labor force thus declined most rapidly in Sweden, less sharply in the United States, the United Kingdom, and Germany, and only very slightly in Switzerland.

For older men, activity rates declined most steeply in the United States: almost 40 percent between 1950 and 1963. The Swedish rate fell by a fourth in the decade of the 1950s alone; the United Kingdom rate fell by almost a fifth, followed by the Swiss rate. Only in Germany did the rate remain approximately the same.

Table 5.2. Labor force participation rates and percentage change in selected countries, by age and sex, 1960–1965

Country	Aged 15–19			Aged 20–64			65 and over			15 and over		
	Total	Men	Women	Total	Men	Women	Total	Men	Women	Total	Men	Women
Federal Republic of Germany [a]												
October, 1958 [b]	76.9	78.9	74.8	66.5	93.1	44.1	14.6	23.4	8.4	60.5	82.8	41.8
April, 1964	69.4	69.6	69.2	67.2	92.7	44.7	14.0	23.5	7.7	58.9	81.2	39.8
Percentage change	− 9.8	−11.8	− 7.5	1.1	− 0.4	1.4	− 4.1	0.0	− 8.3	− 2.6	− 1.9	− 4.8
Sweden [c]												
1950 [d]	64.5	74.4	54.3	63.0	94.7	31.6	20.9	36.1	7.7	57.5	85.8	30.0
1960 [e]	51.9	52.8	49.0	64.6	92.0	37.1	14.9	27.1	4.6	55.7	79.0	32.8
1965 [f]	41.9	46.3	37.2	66.7	88.5	44.0	27.2 [g]	47.8 [g]	8.8 [g]	61.1 [h]	81.2 [h]	40.8 [h]
Percentage change 1950–1960	−19.5	−29.0	− 9.8	2.5	− 2.9	17.4	−28.7	−24.9	−40.3	− 3.1	− 7.9	9.3
Switzerland												
1950	68.8	73.8	64.0	63.8	96.0	34.2	28.4	50.7	11.9	59.8	88.8	33.8
1960	66.2	69.1	63.2	65.9	96.4	36.5	24.0	41.9	11.0	60.5	87.2	35.4
Percentage change	− 3.8	− 6.4	− 1.2	3.3	0.4	6.7	−15.5	−17.4	− 7.6	1.2	− 1.8	4.7
United Kingdom												
1951 [i]	81.2	83.9	78.7	65.2	96.7	36.2	16.0	31.4	5.3	59.6	87.6	34.7
1964 [j]	72.9	72.8	73.1	70.5	96.8	44.7	13.6	25.6	6.1	61.9	85.4	40.3
Percentage change	−10.2	−13.2	− 7.1	8.1	0.1	23.5	−15.0	−18.5	15.1	3.9	− 2.5	16.1

Table 5.2 (*cont.*)

United States [k]											
1950	42.6	53.4	31.5	64.8	94.0	36.5	26.7	45.8	9.7	58.4	84.5	33.1
1963	36.0	43.5	28.4	68.4	94.0	43.9	17.9	28.4	9.6	57.3	78.8	37.0
Percentage change	−15.5	−18.5	−9.8	5.6	0.0	20.3	−33.0	−38.0	−1.0	−1.9	−6.7	11.8

[a] First and last years for which microcensus data (including unemployed) are available for the Federal Republic of Germany including West Berlin.

[b] Excludes the Saar.

[c] Excludes "persons on compulsory military service."

[d] Excludes persons working less than half the normal workday.

[e] Excludes persons working less than half the normal workweek.

[f] Forecasts. Excludes persons working less than half the normal workweek.

[g] Aged 65–69.

[h] Aged 15–69.

[i] Excludes United Kingdom soldiers and merchant seamen stationed overseas.

[j] Forecasts. Excludes foreign merchant seamen and soldiers stationed in the United Kingdom.

[k] Data are for age groups 14–19 and 14 and over. Data from national monthly sample survey of households.

Sources: Germany: *Arbeits- und Sozialstatistische Mitteilungen*, July–August, 1965, p. 172. Sweden: *Tilgangen Pa Arbetskraft 1960–1980*, Statens Offentliga Utredningar, 1966, tables 9, 11. Switzerland: ILO, *Yearbook of Labour Statistics, 1956*, table 2 (Geneva: International Labour Office); United Nations, *Demographic Yearbook, 1962*, table 5 (New York: United Nations). United Kingdom: ILO, *Yearbook of Labour Statistics, 1964*, table 2; *Ministry of Labour Gazette*, January, 1965, p. 4; Central Statistical Office, *Monthly Digest of Statistics*, no. 220 (April, 1964), table 13. United States: United States Department of Labor, *Manpower Report of the President, 1964*, tables A-1, A-2; *1966*, tables A-2, A-7 (Washington: Government Printing Office).

Older women's activity rates also declined very sharply in Sweden; they declined moderately in Germany and Switzerland, remained about the same in the United States, and actually rose in the United Kingdom. The net effect of these changes for older people of both sexes was a decline of about a third in the United States, slightly less in Sweden, approximately 15 percent in the United Kingdom and in Switzerland, and a very small drop in Germany.

In summary, since 1950 the labor force activity of both young and older people has fallen markedly in the United States and Sweden; moderate declines have occurred in the United Kingdom, with much smaller decreases in Switzerland and Germany. In percentage of decline in labor force activity the countries rank from high to low in the following order: aged 15 to 19 (both sexes) —Sweden, United States (14 to 19), United Kingdom, Germany, Switzerland; aged 65 and over (both sexes) —United States, Sweden, Switzerland, United Kingdom, Germany.

Labor Force Activity in the 1960s

Although census reports provide the most nearly comparable figures over a period of time, labor force survey data, when available, give a somewhat better picture of current participation rates. Subject to the qualifications stressed below, the current data indicate the following points of comparison (Table 5.3).[1]

For all ages combined, the participation rates both for men and for men and women combined are lowest in the United States. Following the United States, the male rates are approximately the same for Sweden and Germany (82.6), somewhat higher in the United Kingdom, and highest in Switzerland. The participation rate for women of all ages combined is lowest in Switzerland, followed by the United States, the United Kingdom, Germany, and Sweden. Following the United States low of 57, the combined rate for males and females, all ages, was second lowest for Germany (59.9), which was about the same as that for Switzerland (60.5), and only slightly below the rate for the United Kingdom (61.9). Sweden's high rate (65.4) reflected its high proportion of female workers.

Turning to the proportion of each age group that is active, one finds that men aged 65 and over are labor force participants least frequently in Germany and the United Kingdom, followed by the United States. Switzerland and Sweden have much higher rates. The Swedish proportion, overstated because of the 65–74 base, might well

1. Data are for 1963 except for Switzerland (1960) and United Kingdom (1964). Age groups for United States are 14–19 and 14 and over; for Sweden, 15–74 and 65–74.

Table 5.3. Labor force participation rates in selected countries by age and sex, most recent year available

Country	Year	Aged 15–19			Aged 20–64			65 and over			15 and over		
		Total	Men	Women	Total	Men	Women	Total	Men	Women	Total	Men	Women
Germany	1963	68.2	69.2	67.1	67.7	93.3	45.1	14.6	24.8	8.1	59.9	82.6	40.5
Sweden [a, b]	1963	51.3	52.7	49.7	72.5	90.8	54.1	27.8 [c]	47.0 [c]	11.4 [c]	65.4 [d]	82.0 [d]	48.8 [d]
Switzerland	1960	66.2	69.1	63.2	65.9	96.4	36.5	24.0	41.9	11.0	60.5	87.2	35.4
United Kingdom [e]	1964	72.9	72.8	73.1	70.5	96.8	44.7	13.6	25.6	6.1	61.9	85.4	40.3
United States [a]	1963	36.0 [f]	43.5 [f]	28.4 [f]	68.4	94.0	43.9	17.9 [g]	28.4 [g]	9.6	57.3 [h]	78.8 [h]	37.0 [h]

[a] Based on sample survey.
[b] Excludes persons on compulsory military service.
[c] Aged 65–74. Dividing these data by total population aged 65 and over yields the following rates for the 65 and over group: Total, 18.3; men, 31.4; women, 7.4.
[d] Aged 65–74.
[e] Forecasts.
[f] Aged 14–19.
[g] 1966 participation rate for men aged 65 and over was 27.6.
[h] Aged 14 and over.

Sources: Switzerland, United Kingdom, United States: table 5.2. Germany: *Arbeits- und sozialstatistische Mitteilungen*, May, 1965, p. 107. Sweden: *Tilgangen Pa Arbetskraft 1960–1980*, Statens Offentliga Utredningar, 1966.

be as low as 32 percent (the active persons aged 65–74 divided by the population aged 65 and over), but even then it would rank above all countries except Switzerland. The combined rates for the elderly fall in roughly the same order: the United Kingdom, Germany, the United States, Switzerland, and Sweden.

The participation of male youth is lowest in the United States. Sweden, Switzerland, Germany, and the United Kingdom have significantly higher rates for males aged 15 to 19. Female rates for these age groups fall in the same order, with the result that the countries have combined youth activity rates, from low to high, in the following order: the United States, Sweden, Switzerland, Germany and the United Kingdom.

In summary, the countries rank from low to high in labor force participation rates of young and older men as follows: aged 15 to 19 —United States (14 to 19), Sweden, Switzerland, Germany, United Kingdom; aged 65 and over—Germany, United Kingdom, United States, Switzerland, Sweden (65 to 74).

Low activity rates for male youths have been typical of the United States for some time, but changes in Sweden during recent years account for that country's small proportion of active youth. These two countries have relatively high proportions of older persons at work, despite significant declines during the past decade or so. High activity rates for young men characterize Germany and the United Kingdom, but lower proportions of older males work in these two countries. Switzerland has a relatively high proportion of older men at work and an intermediate figure for young men.

Perhaps the most striking conclusion to be drawn from such a limited comparison is the extent of tradeoff in work during youth (as in Germany and the United Kingdom) for work after age 65 (as in the United States and Sweden). The rapid decline in the participation rates of both young and older men, particularly in the United States and Sweden, suggests that the present rankings may not hold for very long, although participation rates have been somewhat more stable during the postwar period in Germany, Switzerland, and the United Kingdom than in the first two countries.

WORKYEAR COMPARISONS

The length of the workyear, determined by the number of hours worked per week and the number of weeks worked per year, must take into account not only average weekly hours but the amount of time allowed for annual vacations and holidays.

Hours of Work

For data on hours actually worked or even hours paid for (as opposed to standard hours),[2] the most reliable series is for hours worked in manufacturing. This series is used for present purposes, although it is generally recognized that hours in manufacturing are likely to be lower than in certain other sectors, notably agriculture and retail trade.

The United States has a much shorter workweek (40.5) than any of the European countries except Sweden, despite substantial reductions in European schedules during the 1950s and early 1960s (Table 5.4). In West Germany, for example, weekly hours were reduced by three to 44.3 per week, and the workweek in both the United Kingdom, now 43.7, and Switzerland, now 45.5, fell by two hours. No reduction has occurred in the United States during this period.

Table 5.4. Average weekly hours of work in manufacturing, and percentage change in selected countries, 1950 and 1963

Country	Average weekly hours		Percentage change
	1950	1963	
Federal Republic of. Germany [a]	47.4 [b]	44.3 [c]	−6.6
Sweden	41.6	38.5 [d]	−7.8 [e]
Switzerland	47.5	45.5 [c]	−4.2
United Kingdom [f]	45.7	43.7	−4.4
United States [g]	40.5	40.5	0.0

[a] Excludes West Berlin.
[b] 1951 data; includes building and quarrying.
[c] Hours paid for.
[d] 1961 data; includes mining.
[e] Computed from hours of work per month (179 and 165, respectively).
[f] Manual workers.
[g] Production workers; national data from sample survey of employers, relating to persons on payrolls.
Sources: 1950 column and 1963 (except United Kingdom and United States): ILO, *Yearbooks of Labour Statistics, 1956* and *1964*, table 13A (Geneva: International Labour Office). United Kingdom, 1963: *Ministry of Labour Gazette* (November, 1964), p. 456. United States, 1963: *Manpower Report of the President, 1966*, table C-7 (Washington: Government Printing Office). It should be noted that the workweek for Sweden is lower than has been reported elsewhere. See *Labor Relations Abroad*, United States Department of Labor, November, 1968, p. 9, which indicates a workweek of 45 hours for industrial members of the Swedish Trade Union Federation. ILO figures are used here, nevertheless, for consistency of reporting with other countries.

2. The number of hours above which overtime rates become applicable.

Table 5.5. Annual and public holidays with pay in selected countries, 1963 (*in days, except as noted*)

Qualifying period of work	Federal Republic of Germany [a] Statutory and collective agreement	Sweden Statutory	Switzerland [b] Statutory (cantonal)	United Kingdom [c] Statutory and collective agreement	United States [d] Statutory (public holidays) and collective agreement (annual holidays)
Annual holidays					
1–4 years	15	18			5 (1 week)
5–19 years	15	18			10 (2 weeks)
20–24 years	15	18	6–18	12 (2 weeks)	20 (4 weeks)
25–29 years	15	18			20 (4 weeks)
30 or more years	15	18			20 (4 weeks)
Paid public holidays	10–13	11	8	6	6

[a] Generally supplemented by collective agreement.
[b] 1962 data.
[c] Statutory minimum is 14 days, breakdown by qualifying period not available; by collective agreement, 3–4 weeks (qualifying period ranges from 5 to 35 years).
[d] Extensions by collective bargaining.

Sources: "Labour Overseas," *Ministry of Labour Gazette*, February, 1962, p. 59; November, 1964, p. 456; Dr. Hans Reithafer, "How Much Holiday for Europe's Workers," *Free Labour World*, July–August, 1963; ILO, *Annual Holidays with Pay* (Geneva: International Labour Office, 1964); William Gerber, "Time Off with Pay in the United Kingdom," unpublished paper.

Annual and Public Holidays

Examination of paid vacations and holidays in the various countries again reveals widely different patterns (Table 5.5). Sweden has the most generous provision for annual vacations (18 days) and in addition allows 11 public holidays. Sweden is followed by Germany, with a total of 25 to 28 days free; Switzerland, with 14 to 26 days depending on the canton; and the United Kingdom with 18 days. Probably the most frequent arrangement for workers in the United States is the 2-week, or 10-day annual vacation, which can go up to 4 weeks with extended length of service plus 6 paid holidays—a total of 16 days.

Length of the Workyear

For the full-time factory worker in the various countries, very rough estimates can be made of the number of hours worked per year (see Figure 5.1). In Sweden the short workweek means that the

Figure 5.1. Length of workyear in selected countries, recent years

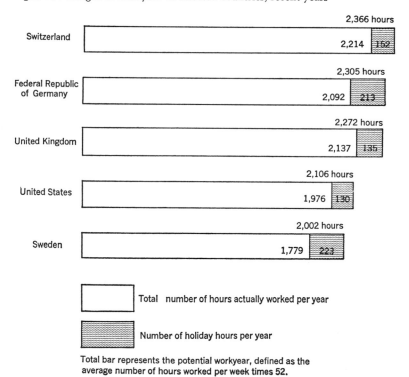

Total number of hours actually worked per year

Number of holiday hours per year

Total bar represents the potential workyear, defined as the average number of hours worked per week times 52.

workyear would be low even with no holidays (38.5 hours for 52 weeks, or 2,002 hours). After deducting 29 holidays (or 5.8 weeks × 38.5 hours), the average workyear is about 1,779 hours. Similar computations yield a workyear of 1,976 hours for the United States (40.5 hours per week for 52 weeks, or 2,106 hours, less 3.2 weeks for vacations and holidays); 2,092 hours for West Germany (44.3 hours for 52 weeks, less 15 vacation days and 11.5 public holidays, totaling 4.8 weeks or 213 hours); 2,137 for the United Kingdom (43.7 hours for 52 weeks, less 87.4 hours for annual and 48 hours for public holidays); and for Switzerland, 2,214 (45.5 hours for 52 weeks, less 20 days or 3.33 weeks for annual and public holidays).

The range between Sweden's short and Switzerland's long workyear is thus more than 400 hours, or about 10 weeks annually. Of the three intermediate countries, the United States stands about midway between the two extremes set by Sweden and Switzerland, while Germany and the United Kingdom have workyears which more nearly approach that of Switzerland.

VARIATIONS IN LEISURE TIME PATTERNS

Data on the amount of leisure may be illuminated by further analysis of the forms this leisure takes in the various countries. The following country-by-country discussion sketches the current patterns of nonworking time and points up recent changes in the amount of leisure appearing in any particular form.

Germany

In recent decades, German workers have had a high labor force participation rate in youth and a relatively low activity rate in old age. Of the five countries reviewed, Germany has the lowest proportion of elderly men at work. The manufacturing employee in Germany works several hours more per week than the Swedish or United States worker, but again there is an offset: a great many days for annual and public holidays. As a result of the long workweek and the generous holiday arrangements, the German worker's annual hours fall in an intermediate position, with hours in Sweden and the United States lower and those in the United Kingdom and Switzerland higher. Germany's workweek has fallen substantially during the past decade, and there is every indication of continued pressure toward a 40-hour week. Comments by labor and industry spokesmen have indicated that a shorter workweek has some priority over an increase in alternative forms of leisure. There is no evidence of a desire for increase in leisure in the form of retirement and no apparent move for reducing retirement age.

United Kingdom

Both men and women in the United Kingdom have exceptionally high labor force participation rates as teenagers but relatively low rates in old age. The high participation rates for young people in 1964 nevertheless represent a substantial decrease from the 1951 level; the combined participation rate for this age group fell from 81 in 1950 to 73 in 1964. This pattern of change was quite similar to that in the United States, and the resemblance between the two countries is even more striking in the 20–64 age groups. In both countries the male rate was stabilized at a high level: 97 percent in the United Kingdom and 94 percent in the United States. On the other hand, women in both countries significantly increased their economic activity, the rates in the United Kingdom rising by 24 percent and those in the United States by 20 percent. For aged men in the United Kingdom, participation rates, which were relatively low, have fallen only moderately during the past decade, and the participation of older women has actually increased.

There are also similarities between the United States and the United Kingdom in workyear patterns. Vacation allowances are practically the same in the two countries, and each provides 6 public holidays. The United Kingdom workweek of 43.7 hours, although down by 2 hours from its 1950 level, remains substantially longer than that in the United States.

Sweden

Both the amount of leisure and its allocation over the worklife in Sweden differ significantly from the patterns in other countries. Swedish youth aged 15 to 19 have the lowest participation rate among the European countries; men aged 65 and over have relatively high rates, however. Women in Sweden have the lowest teenage labor force rates in the European countries studied, but their participation rates during the 20–64 age period is the highest of all countries, including the United States. It is obvious that the Swedish woman is likely to stay in the labor force even during the years when family responsibilities are heaviest. The extremely high female rate in this age group is more than sufficient to offset the very low rate for men of prime working age, giving Sweden the highest combined rate of any of the countries studied.

The short workweek is accompanied by frequent paid holidays and extremely generous annual holidays. In 1963 the weekly hours for men in manufacturing were shorter in Sweden than in the other countries, and the rate of decline in hours was much faster there than elsewhere. In 1965 annual holidays increased from 18 to 24; collective agreements add to this vacation period. Swedish men thus have a short workyear, enter the labor force late, and retire late. The heavy labor force participation of women, following much the same pattern in the timing of worklife, serves to spread nonworking time between the sexes more evenly than in the other countries.

Switzerland

The participation rate for Swiss men is higher than for men in the other countries; this was also true in 1950. Unlike those in other countries, the male activity rates are high for all three age groups: 15–19, 20–64, and 65 and over. Among women, teenagers and those in the 20–64 age group are in the labor force less frequently, on the whole, than their counterparts in other countries, but the participation rate for older women is high. Changes in Swiss activity rates over the decade of the 1950s follow much the same pattern as in other countries, at least with respect to direction. However, the magnitude of change was relatively small for all groups of workers except aged men.

The Swiss workweek is also high; however, this figure is for hours paid for and therefore probably overstates working time somewhat. Weekly hours are thus not too different from hours worked in West Germany and the United Kingdom. The decline in hours has been significant, approaching the relative decline in the United Kingdom. Annual holidays vary widely by canton. In Geneva the 18 days provided by law compares favorably with holiday time in most other countries; as to public holidays, the 8-day pattern ranks Switzerland midway among the countries.

United States

During the two decades following World War II, weekly hours for United States workers in nonagricultural industries have fallen only slightly; the major gains in workweek reduction occurred early in the century. Paid vacations, on the other hand, have grown in both coverage and length during the postwar period. Although pressure for further reductions in hours worked per week occasionally appears, there is equally strong opposition to any nationwide movement in this direction, particularly if it involves statutory changes.[3] Further growth in vacation time seems more likely, its provision being by voluntary agreement rather than through legislation. American workers at present enjoy a significantly shorter workweek than Germany, the United Kingdom, or Switzerland, but fewer annual and public holidays than the European nations other than the United Kingdom.

In changing patterns of working life, the United States somewhat resembles the Swedish direction. Participation rates for men have declined, and those for women have increased. Moreover, in these two countries males enter the labor force later than elsewhere. But there are important differences. In Sweden the high proportion of working women of all ages is partially offset by greatly reduced working hours per week and increased holiday time; in the United States, women's increased labor force activity has been counterbalanced by the reduced participation of both younger and older men.

3. For discussions of proposed statutory reduction in working hours, see references cited in n. 12, chap. 2, above.

6. INCOME AND LEISURE ISSUES IN ADVANCED ECONOMIES

The distribution of lifetime between working years and leisure years apparently depends primarily on the nation's stage of economic development, or more precisely, on the productivity of labor and hence the extent to which nonworking time can be supported. Evidence cited earlier indicates that labor force activity rates for males are highest in agricultural and lowest in industrialized countries. The downward trend among the industrially advanced nations continues, moreover, with the major declines appearing at the beginning and at the end of the worklife span. Since mid-century, the rates of decline in the activity of young men have differed among the five countries surveyed, as have the rates for men aged 65 and over; yet the overall effect has been to increase the number of nonworking years for men in all of these countries.

The scientific and technological progress that increases productivity per manhour also increases life expectancy, with the result that both working and nonworking years have increased during the twentieth century. Male worklife expectancy in the United States saw its first downturn in the decade of the 1950s, but the number of years spent outside the labor force has grown throughout the century, and it seems likely that additional years of life will henceforth be allocated to education, training, and retirement rather than to work.

This chapter reviews some of the evidence of an inverse relation between income level and amount of work performed, in terms of both workyear and worklife, and considers the levels of income maintained during retirement years. Despite high average earnings, the levels of income maintained in nonworking periods tend to be quite low. Differences between earnings and retirement income tend to increase, moreover, unless retirement incomes reflect the process of economic growth.

THE INVERSE RELATION BETWEEN INCOME AND WORK

Inactive years for men are few in underdeveloped countries, as John D. Durand noted a decade and a half ago. Rurality and low incomes, he suggested, were the major reasons for high activity rates in those countries; hence the appearance of nonagricultural industries, the growth of cities, and increases in output per worker should lead to a decline in the labor force activity of men at both ends of working life.[1] The data presented in the preceding chapters, although far from satisfactory as precise measures of differences among the countries, nevertheless bear out Durand's earlier thesis. Irene Taeuber's work on Japanese demographic patterns reveals even more clearly than the European data a downward trend in activity rates for young and older men in the 1920–1940 period, despite Japan's wartime mobilization. Among the 10–14-year-olds the economically active percentage fell from 20.6 to 10.1 during these two decades, and the participation of men in the 15–19, the 55–59, and the 60-and-over age groups also declined substantially.[2]

The tendency for growth in productivity and real income to be accompanied by increasing amounts of time free of work has been noted often, but rarely has attention been given to international comparisons of income and work. Winston's recent study, however, addressing itself to the question whether as incomes rise people systematically change their distribution of time between work and leisure, employs aggregate international cross-sectional data. The author concludes from the international data that there is a significant negative correlation between income and the aggregate allocation of effort to income acquisition, and that the values of the

1. "Population Structure as a Factor in Manpower and Dependency Problems," p. 10. The author concluded also that male labor force activity rates in the more highly developed sections of some of the underdeveloped countries resembled the activity patterns in the industrially advanced countries. Urbanization thus has a particularly pronounced tendency to lower the participation rates for young and old males.

2. Irene B. Taeuber, *The Population of Japan* (Princeton, N.J.: Princeton University Press, 1958).

estimated relationship are strikingly similar to those from earlier studies using intercity and industry cross-sectional data on occupational subgroups within societies.[3]

As the indicator of the amount of effort devoted to income acquisition, Winston uses hours worked per capita, which is the product of average hours worked and the rate of labor force participation. For the latter, two measures are employed: one, the participation rate for persons aged 14 and over, standardized for population composition, and two, the participation rate for men of prime working age, 20 to 64. For hours of work, again, alternatives are used: average hours per week, using aggregate-hours data, and average hours in manufacturing. Regardless of the combination of hours and participation rates, the negative relationship between income and social effort was maintained. For example, the fully aggregated data (the standardized participation rate multiplied by general hours) regressed against per capita national income indicate a highly significant negative relationship (at the 0.5 percent level). The value of the regression coefficient would indicate a 1.074 percent reduction in per capita working time with a 10 percent increase in per capita real income. In the case of one underdeveloped country, the author points out that if such a relationship held for Peru, a doubling of its per capita income ($125 in 1957) would be accompanied by a per capita decline of 135 working hours per year.

Of the variables other than income that explain the allocation of effort, the most important, Winston concludes, is the state of aggregate demand as indicated by the level of unemployment. Positive deviations from the fitted regression occur in countries with low levels of unemployment, while negative deviations appear in cases of high unemployment levels. It is interesting to note the relation of the two variables, per capita national income and level of unemployment, to social effort in the five countries under scrutiny. The United States has by far the highest income; it has also suffered the greatest unemployment. Germany, Switzerland, the United Kingdom, and Sweden have lower income and lower unemployment levels than the United States.[4]

Although generalizations are somewhat hazardous, it does appear that the high income–high unemployment position of the United States has lessened the amount of effort allocated to work. Questions

3. Gordon C. Winston, "An International Comparison of Income and Hours of Work," *Review of Economics and Statistics,* 48 (February, 1966), 28, 38.
   4. Ibid., p. 35.

may well be posed for those European countries whose productivity and income levels are rising rapidly: How successfully will a portion of their higher standards of living be translated into greater leisure, including retirement? Will they be able to make the transfer more smoothly, avoiding the unemployment problem that has constituted perhaps the primary pressure for the growth of leisure in the United States?

INCOME LEVELS AND WORK IN OLD AGE

International comparisons of income levels can be drawn from either per capita income data or from wage rates in the different countries. In the United Kingdom, Germany, and Switzerland the general wage per hour is less than half that in the United States; even the Swedish general wage is only two-thirds the United States

Table 6.1. Average hourly earnings [a] for men in selected countries, 1957 and 1964

Country	1957		1964	
	General	Manufac-turing	General	Manufac-turing
Federal Republic of Germany	$0.562	$0.551	$1.045	$1.025
Sweden	1.039 [b]	1.031	1.550 [b]	1.482
Switzerland	0.707	0.717	1.080	1.064
United Kingdom	0.730	0.761	1.062	1.11
United States	1.90 [b]	2.05 [c]	2.30 [b]	2.53 [c]

[a] Derived from rates reported in local currency by the International Labour Office and converted to United States currency at the exchange rates reported by ILO.

[b] General wage level not reported. Entry computed by weighting sectoral wage levels reported by ILO and Bureau of Labor Statistics by sectoral distribution of the labor force. However, data were not complete and may not be comparable to the other entries in these columns. In addition, computed rate is for both men and women.

[c] Rate for both men and women, which thus understates the male rate.

Sources: ILO, *Yearbook of Labour Statistics, 1965,* tables 18, 19A, 20–22 (Geneva: International Labour Office); United Nations, *Statistical Yearbook, 1962,* tables 39, 67; *1965,* tables 53, 82, 139 (New York: United Nations); United States Department of Labor, *Monthly Labor Review,* December, 1958, tables A-2, C-1; November, 1966, tables A-9, C-1.

rate (Table 6.1). Rapid growth in output in West Germany, which in the earlier year had the lowest per capita income, nevertheless raised that nation's income per person to only 52 percent of the United States level for 1964 (Table 6.2). The United Kingdom had

Table 6.2. Per capita gross domestic product and national income in selected countries, 1957 and 1964 (*current dollars*)

Country	Per capita gross domestic product at factor cost		Per capita national income	
	1957	1964	1957	1964
Federal Republic of Germany	$ 837	$1,541	$ 741	$1,409
Sweden	1,273	2,013	— a	— a
Switzerland	1,308	2,003	1,220	1,815
United Kingdom	1,039	1,472	955	1,275
United States	2,345	3,002	2,110	2,696

a National income data not available in United Nations sources.

Sources: United Nations, *Yearbook of National Accounts Statistics, 1958*, table 1; *1965*, tables 1, 9A; *Statistical Yearbook, 1958*, table 1; *1965*, table 19 (New York: United Nations).

slower economic growth during the period and consequently had achieved a per capita income only 47 percent of that in the United States in 1964. Income in the United States thus continued to be one and a half to two times as high as the income in the other countries, despite recent differences in rates of growth.[5]

In contrast to the much higher per capita incomes and wage rates in the United States, the proportion of earned income maintained for persons in retirement in this country is relatively low (Table 6.3). The Federal Republic of Germany, which has next to the lowest per capita national income, assures the highest proportion of average wages to old-age recipients. These benefits are payable, moreover, without regard to whether the older person has retired. Sweden's average benefit is also a substantially higher proportion of average

5. Index numbers of total and per capita product at constant prices are as follows (1958 = 100):

Country	Total product		Per capita product	
	1957	1964	1957	1964
Federal Republic of Germany	97	141	98	131
Sweden	99	135	99	130
Switzerland	102	140	103	124
United Kingdom	100	124	101	119
United States	101	129	103	117

Source: United Nations, *Statistical Yearbook, 1965* (New York: United Nations, 1966), table 179.

Table 6.3. Average old-age benefits as a percentage of average wages in manufacturing and pensionable age, in selected countries, most recent year available

Country	Year		Average benefits as a percentage of average wages for all workers	Normal pensionable age [a]	
	Benefits	Wages		Men	Women
Federal Republic of Germany	1963 [b]	1963 [c]	31.4	65	65
Sweden	1962 [d]	1961–1962	22.4	67	67
Switzerland	1963 [e]	1963 [f]	18.0	65	62
United Kingdom	1965 [g]	1965	15.2	65	60
United States	1964 [h]	1964	18.2	65	65

[a] Earlier retirement, under varying conditions, is provided in most countries.

[b] June.

[c] May; includes family allowances paid directly by employer.

[d] January; old-age pensions.

[e] Old-age and survivor payments.

[f] Adult male (skilled and unskilled) and all women workers weighted by the number of persons in each category.

[h] Retirement pensions.

[g] Old-age, survivor, and disability awards.

Sources: Germany: Georg Tietz's summary of data in *Zalenwerk zur Sozialversicherung* (Berlin, 1963). Sweden: *Statistisk Arsbok for Sverige, 1964*, tables 253, 272. Switzerland: *Statistisches Jahrbuch der Schweiz, 1965*, pp. 296, 371. United Kingdom: *Report of the Ministry of Pensions and National Insurance for the Year 1965*, pp. 78, 132; *Ministry of Labour Gazette*, August, 1965, p. 525. United States: United States Department of Health, Education, and Welfare, *Social Security Bulletin*, March, 1966, table Q-6; United States Department of Commerce, *Survey of Current Business*, July, 1966, pp. S-14, S-15. Pensionable age: United States Department of Health, Education, and Welfare, *Social Security Programs Throughout the World, 1967* (Washington: Government Printing Office, 1967).

wages than is our own retirement benefit; pensionable age is also later.

The relation between average earnings and retirement benefits would seem to be more relevant to the retirement decision of an individual than earnings as such, at least when full employment prevails and retirement is optional within the age range of, say, 65 to 69.[6] In the case of West Germany, the lower participation rate

6. In an earlier study Margaret Gordon ("Income Security Programs and the Propensity to Retire," in Richard H. Williams, Clark Tibbitts, and Wilma Donahue, eds., *Processes of Aging*, New York: Atherton, 1963, pp. 436–458) computed coefficients between "benefit rates" (ratio of average benefits to average annual earnings) and the proportion of men 65 and over in the labor force for 14 countries, using data for old-age, survivors, and invalidity (OASI) benefit programs, and for 9 countries, using data for old age (OA) only. Coefficients were −.83 and −.78, indicating that "a substantial proportion of the variation in labor force participation rates of elderly men in industrialized countries is associated with differences in

Table 6.4. Labor force participation rates for men aged 65–69 in selected countries, recent years

Country	1950	1960	1964
Federal Republic of Germany	26.8 [a]	33.2 [b]	36.6
Sweden:			
Census (excluding unemployed)	56.4	50.6	47.8 [c]
Survey	— [d]	58.6	48.5
Switzerland	65.9	59.2	— [d]
United Kingdom	48.7 [e]	39.5 [f]	39.6 [g]
United States	59.8	43.8	42.6

[a] Aged 65 and over; excludes West Berlin.
[b] 1961 data; excludes West Berlin.
[c] 1965 data.
[d] Not available.
[e] 1951 data.
[f] 1961 data.
[g] Forecast.

Sources: 1950 and 1960 columns: United Nations, *Demographic Year-book, 1955,* table 15; 1964, table 8 (New York: United Nations). 1964 column: Germany: *Arbeits und sozialstatistische Mitteilungen,* July–August, 1965, p. 172. Sweden: *Tilgangen Pa Arbetskraft 1960–1980,* Statens Offentliga Utredningar, 1966, tables 6, 9. United Kingdom: *Ministry of Labour Gazette,* January, 1965, p. 4; Central Statistical Office, *Monthly Digest of Statistics,* no. 220 (April, 1964), table 13. United States: United States Department of Labor, *The Older American Worker,* June, 1965, p. 145.

of men in this age group bears out this hypothesis (Table 6.4). Swedish figures are not comparable, since pensionable age is 67, and the proportion of older men at work in the United Kingdom is

benefit ratios." Her data on the 5 countries reviewed in the present study show the following relationships for 1950 and 1957:

Country	Percentage of men 65 and over in labor force	Average benefit as percentage of annual earnings		Average benefit (OASDI) as percentage of national income per capita	
		OASI	OA	1950	1957
Federal Republic of Germany	26.8	22	—	55	60
Sweden	36.1	16	15	28	38
Switzerland	50.7	9	10	14	19
United Kingdom	31.4	18	18	28	27
United States	41.4	14	15	18	41

For differences in benefits as a percentage of annual earnings as shown in table 6.3, see notes on table 6.3 and the basis of computations made by Gordon, ("Income Security Programs and the Propensity to Retire," pp. 444–446, 451). Note also that data are for different years.

slightly lower than that in the United States, despite the somewhat larger proportion of earnings maintained in the latter country.

Examination of the pension–earnings ratios in other countries may reveal a direct relation between the ratio and the proportion of men who retire in the five-year span following pensionable age. But such comparisons are hazardous for several reasons: measures of part-time work in old age, which are crucial to such analysis, are poor; the data on other sources of income of the elderly are sparse except for older people in the United States; [7] and finally, there is considerable variation in the practice of using a retirement test as a condition of drawing pensions. [8]

Although the relevant group would seem to be men aged 65–69 for countries with pensionable age of 65, this age group typically has the highest incomes among the elderly because of continued work and higher benefits. The lower benefit levels accrue to men aged 70 and over, older women of all ages, and, in the United States, to retired men aged 62 to 64 whose characteristics often suggest that the pension is a form of unemployment compensation. Pension incentives probably have little to do with the act of retirement in such cases; retirement is not optional but is a product of economic circumstances which for the older group seem unlikely to change. For the early retirees in the United States the recent shift in economic climate may be more promising.

PENSIONABLE AGE AND THE AGE OF RETIREMENT

An inverse relation between average earnings and time spent at work has been demonstrated, using international cross-sectional data. Similarly, an inverse relation between the proportion of earnings maintained as pension and the labor force participation of men in the early years of eligibility might well be shown if reliable data were available. However, the influence of normal pensionable age on actual retirement age is obviously of primary significance, despite variations in pension arrangements among various countries. It is important to note the extent to which actual retirement age has come to approach pensionable age, and then to examine the factors

7. See Lenore A. Epstein and Janet H. Murray, *The Aged Population of the United States,* Department of Health, Education, and Welfare, Social Security Administration Report 19, 1967.

8. T. Higuchi, "Old-Age Pensions and Retirement," *International Labour Review,* 90 (October, 1964), 1–19.

that account for the establishment of, or a change in, pensionable age.

In a recent survey, more than one-third of the responding nations stated that the average exact age of initial receipt of pension was either the same as or within one year of normal pensionable age, i.e., the earliest age at which normal old-age pension becomes payable. When there were differences between pensionable and actual retirement age the latter was higher, but for schemes having 65 as the pensionable age the variation was generally small. The observance of a "normal" retirement age is noteworthy, particularly in view of the availability of advanced pensions in more than half of the countries; many of these advanced pensions were not reduced.[9]

Deferred retirement credits are also available in 24 of the 57 schemes covered in the report, but there is not sufficient evidence to demonstrate that a delayed retirement credit induces workers to postpone retirement, even when the amount of the increment is substantial. The role played by a retirement test is also unclear. Thirty-seven schemes imposed some sort of retirement condition, ranging from the stipulation that the worker give up all remunerative work to less stringent rules, such as limitations on earnings up to a specified age. With only one exception, the 20 schemes having no retirement test were content with their arrangements, whereas almost half the 37 having such tests reported some sentiment for changing the regulations. The estimated costs of eliminating the retirement condition ran from "negligible" in Italy to a 40 percent increase in Jersey (C.I.). The estimated long-run rise in cost in the United States was 10 percent.[10]

Higher costs resulting from removal of a retirement test would presumably be more than offset by an increase in the total output of the larger labor force. If the state of the economy called for additional manpower and retirees constituted a potential labor source, waiving the retirement test could be justified, since it would furnish the inducement for older persons to remain in the labor force. The three countries in the present study with the tightest labor markets

9. Alvin M. David, "Problems of Retirement Age and Related Conditions for the Receipt of Old-Age Benefits," Report 9 of the Fifteenth General Assembly, *Bulletin of the International Social Security Association,* 17 (February–April, 1965), 97–109.

10. Ibid., pp. 105–106. The author concludes: "The literature indicates that there is a relationship, in a given country, between the existence of provisions requiring a pensioner to retire from paid or insurable employment or to limit his earnings in order to receive his pension, the nature and purpose of the old-age scheme itself, the economic conditions prevailing in the country and the proportion of the gross national product that is made available for social security programmes. However, it has not been possible to confirm that such relationships exist" (p. 105).

impose no retirement provision. In Sweden, entitlement to benefits does not depend on financial participation of the worker or on any qualifying period; the scheme is tax financed and allows concurrent receipt of both wages and benefits. Switzerland and the Federal Republic of Germany have social insurance schemes in which the pension is again not contingent upon retirement or income. Moreover, the German worker may claim an advanced pension at age 60 or afterward if he has been unemployed for a year and is unlikely to find work. The United Kingdom and the United States apply earnings tests up to age 70 and 72, respectively.

The tendency for actual retirement age to approach pensionable age is easy to understand in an economy of labor excess. The bidding for limited jobs must either force some of the workers out of jobs or push down the wage rate; the latter would require considerably more downward flexibility of wages and prices than has actually prevailed in the postwar economy in the United States. Thus, those workers who have pensions are expected to vacate their jobs in favor of younger men who have not only better education and more up-to-date skills but also greater financial needs. It is precisely the logic of this retirement-on-schedule pattern that compels attention to any movement toward a lowering of pensionable age, or even any increase in the prevalence of early retirement provisions in private pension schemes. The question whether the age at which one *may* retire is to become the age at which one is *expected* to retire must be kept clearly in mind.

RETIREMENT POLICY AND MANPOWER NEEDS

The imposition of a retirement condition and the selection of pensionable age itself are of course likely to reflect the policy-maker's view of the manpower situation. One of the major considerations in the establishment of old-age benefits in the United States was the intent of drawing elderly persons off the labor market and thus helping to restore the balance between the supply of and demand for labor. It followed that the benefit would have to be contingent on actual retirement. The lowering of pensionable age for men further recognized the need to provide income for men aged 62 to 64 who for reasons other than disability could no longer find employment. But perhaps the clearest example of the relation between manpower problems and retirement policy is the pension scheme negotiated by the United Automobile Workers. Here, the need to remove excess labor from a rapidly automating industry led to extremely generous private pensions, permitting workers to retire as early as 55.

In contrast, the nations of Western Europe have attempted to keep older persons at work, and the advantages of a flexible retirement age are frequently cited.[11] Although pensionable age clusters at 65 for both men and women in the member countries of the Organization for Economic Cooperation and Development, inducements to continue working, such as West Germany's scheme for increasing the size of the pension if retirement is postponed, are frequent. In Sweden the pensionable age is 67, with provisions for a 0.6 percent reduction for every month the pension is taken prior to that age, down to 63; a similar increment is added for each month beyond age 67 that the pension is postponed. In Great Britain the newly introduced graduated pension, not being subject to a retirement test, may provide some incentive to work beyond age 65.

Although convincing arguments are being made for flexible retirement age in European countries suffering labor shortages, there has been no attempt to raise pensionable age. It is understandable that there is also no movement to lower the age of retirement, given the need for manpower. Curiously, while incentives are being offered to keep older workers at work, there is strong pressure for shortening the workweek and lengthening annual vacations. Moreover, there are many inducements to bring women into the labor force: child care centers, special arrangements for rest periods on the job, and extensive maternity and sick leave provisions.

These attempts to serve manpower needs by increasing the number of workers, while still allowing each employee gradually to reduce his workyear, are in direct contrast to the situation in the United States, both as to manpower needs and the manner of meeting these needs. Here, demographic developments have been markedly different. The population of working age has been growing rapidly and will continue to do so; comparable data on the increase in the United States and in European nations, summarized in OECD studies, are shown in Table 6.5.

In addition to the United States' greater increase in the numbers of persons of labor-force age, the nation's technological pace has re-

11. See, for example, Sven O. Hyden, *Flexible Retirement Age* (Paris: Organization for Economic Cooperation and Development, 1966). Other OECD studies dealing with retirement and older-worker problems are: A. Heron, *Age and Employment* (1962); Stephen Griew, *Job Re-design* (1964); R. M. Belbin, *Training Methods* (1965); Irvin Sobel and Richard Wilcock, *Placement Techniques for Older Workers* (1965); Bert Andersen, *Work or Support* (1966) and *The Employment of Older Workers* (1965).

Table 6.5. Percentage increases in population of working age, 1966–1976

0–4	5–9	10–14	15–19	20–29
Austria	France	Netherlands	United States	Turkey
Belgium	Norway	Portugal		
Denmark				
Germany				
Ireland				
Italy				
Sweden				
Switzerland				
United Kingdom				

duced the demand for labor per unit of output, thereby creating a further labor market imbalance. The solution to this imbalance has resulted in growth of leisure in a form that differs from any added free time in the European nations. Here, the labor force has been reduced at both ends of the worklife span. Despite the fact that our age of entry into the labor force has traditionally been much later than in European nations, the movement toward further postponement continues here, with Sweden the only close competitor in number of years of schooling provided youth.

The allocation of a substantial portion of the growth in leisure to the retirement period has the advantage of making the free time available to all workers who survive to retirement age. Conceivably, leisure in the form of extended vacations might be somewhat less evenly apportioned over the labor force, accruing, initially at least, most generously to workers whose bargaining strength enables them to gain contractual concessions providing for reduced working time.[12] Moreover, there is the broader question of the practicability of trade-off between retirement leisure and vacation (or other workyear) arrangements; there are certain difficulties involved in reapportioning the available nonworking time. Finally, we know very little about workers' actual preferences as to the distribution of free time. The question whether increased leisure in old age is in fact preferred directs attention to a consideration of the broader issue of the allocation of future leisure, which promises to grow rapidly. Evidence that other advanced countries are choosing patterns of leisure time somewhat different from our own underscores the importance of discerning actual preferences before policy is established.

12. The author is indebted to Robert L. Stein, formerly of the Office of Research and Statistics, Social Security Administration, for raising this question and making other valuable criticisms.

7. POTENTIAL GROWTH AND ALLOCATION OF LEISURE IN THE UNITED STATES

LEISURE, PRESENT AND FUTURE

The amount of free time promises to grow even greater in the United States as technology continues to raise productivity per man-hour. As earlier estimates indicated (see chapter 2), today's employed worker has about 1,200 hours per year more nonworking time than his 1890 counterpart. The additional free time is apportioned over the year in the following forms: reduction in workweek (from 61.9 to 40.5 hours), approximately 1,100 hours; increase in paid holidays (4 days), 32 hours; increase in paid vacation (6 days), 48 hours; increase in sick leave (1 week), 40 hours. Reductions in the workweek have thus been the major source of additional free time during worklife. In addition to a shortened workyear, nonworking years have grown by about 9 for a male at birth, with present life and worklife expectancies; this increase amounts to about one-third the free time added to each workyear.[1]

With regard to the possible future growth in leisure and its probable distribution, rough estimates have been made on the basis of anticipated rates of economic growth, population increase, and unemployment levels and under varying assumptions regarding preferences as to the distribution of time between work and leisure. At one extreme, assuming no change in working time, per capita gross

1. This chapter is taken from Kreps and Spengler, "The Leisure Component of Economic Growth," op. cit. For source see the summary data of estimates in Ewan Clague in *Hours of Work*, Part I, pp. 73–104; also other sources cited above (chap. 2, n. 12).

national product could rise from $3,181 in 1965 to $5,802 in 1985, or by about 80 percent. At the other extreme, if one supposes that all growth is taken in leisure time except the amount necessary to keep per capita GNP constant at $3,181, the possible changes in working time would be as follows: the workweek could fall to 22 hours, or the workyear could be limited to 27 weeks per year, or retirement age could be lowered to 38 years, or almost half the labor

Figure 7.1. Alternative uses of economic growth per capita gross national product and hours worked, 1965–1985

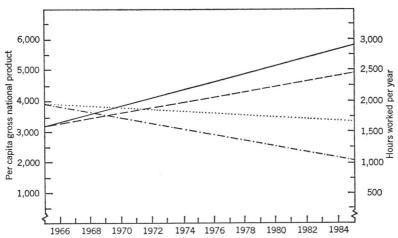

———— Per capita GNP with constant workyear

– – – – Per capita GNP with two-thirds of projected growth taken in income, one-third in leisure

············ Length of workyear with two-thirds of projected growth taken in income, one-third in leisure

–·–·– Length of workyear with constant per capita GNP

Source: GNP projections and employment data from National Planning Association, Report no. 65–1, March, 1965. Labor force data for other computations taken from Manpower Report of the President, March, 1965, p. 248, table E-2.

force could be kept in retraining programs, or additional time available for education might well exceed our capacity to absorb such education (Figure 7.1).

More realistically, it might be supposed that the division of productivity gains would be approximately the same as during the first half of the century: two-thirds in increased goods and one-third in time free of work. Then per capita GNP would rise to approximately $5,000 by 1985, and the short-run growth in leisure would be sufficient to achieve the following goals: retrain 1 percent of the labor force annually and increase vacation time by one week for each worker. These goals, attained during roughly the first 15 years, could then be followed by a decline of, say, half an hour per week starting in the early 1970s; the decline reaching two hours and a half per week by 1980. Between 1980 and 1985 society could choose to retrain much more heavily (4.25 percent of the labor force per year) or add a week and a half per year to vacation time. By 1985, the choice could be between retraining almost 7 percent of the labor force annually and taking an additional 3 weeks of vacation. Obviously, other choices are possible.[2]

In summary, the amount of time free of work in the United States not only has grown rapidly during this century but is also destined to expand to much greater dimensions in the coming decade. What forms this new leisure will take are of great significance—as important, perhaps, as the composition of the goods produced. A greater amount of free time at the end of worklife is but one of several forms in which leisure could be allocated. Its desirability over other forms of free time, moreover, is in part dependent on the financial arrangements made for the retirement period.

THE PROBLEM OF RETIREMENT INCOME

To the extent that the growth in nonworking time takes the form of a shortened workyear, the cost of the leisure, measured in terms of product foregone, is concealed in the wage-price relationship, and income maintenance arrangements are not affected. Recent increases in leisure in the European nations, being apportioned largely in shorter workweeks and longer vacations, have not magnified the problem of income maintenance in old age. Tight labor markets, moreover, have encouraged the utilization of older persons who cared to continue working. In the United States, by contrast, the level of unemployment during the past two decades has led industry and Congress to make early retirement possible. Meanwhile, few incentives have been offered to induce continued labor force participation past the age of 65.

As F. LeGros Clark has pointed out, the acceptance of 65 as the age of withdrawal from work occurred earlier in the United States than in the United Kingdom; further, an inching down below age

2. Kreps and Spengler, "The Leisure Component of Economic Growth," pp. 363–365.

65 has now begun in this country.[3] Whether such a movement will continue here and develop in other nations as their income levels approach our own is difficult to predict. Nevertheless, it is clear that certain retirement-related problems are peculiar to the United States, if for no other reason than the fact that we reached a certain level of economic development somewhat earlier than other countries.

Perhaps the best indicator of this nation's economic advance is its faster pace of technology and the resultant acceleration of real incomes during the past two decades. Higher postwar rates of economic growth in Western Europe have narrowed but by no means eliminated the United States' lead in per capita income. Paradoxically, the higher the per capita income rises, the more acute become the income problems of certain groups of people, i.e., those groups who are not current participants in the economic process. For the higher income reflects higher productivity per manhour, and such increases in our economy are expected to accrue to the workers who are actually at work, rather than to those of the preceding or succeeding generation of workers.

Considerable disparity between income during working years and retirement years may be quite acceptable in an economy that places great stress on the output of the individual worker. Job performance supposedly is rewarded by a wage roughly commensurate with productivity; in fact, the promise of higher income provides the incentive for greater worker effort. Given a wage structure explained largely in terms of output per manhour, it is easy to develop a rationale for variations in wages for different jobs (or individual performances on a particular job), a gradual decline in income if productivity declines with age, and a still lower assured income during retirement.

The social security program justifies a transfer of income from workers to nonworkers on the basis of previous earnings and contributions. The essence of the retirement benefit—the transfer of income claims from workers to nonworkers—is not always recognized, however. That such a transfer is necessary may also be obscured, and the range of options as to methods of transfer may not be systematically explored. Intergenerational transfers of income, once made within families, have come increasingly to be made between workers and nonworkers, irrespective of family ties,[4] and the

3. Frederick LeGros Clark, *Work, Age, and Leisure* (London: Michael Joseph, 1966), p. 137.
4. Juanita M. Kreps, "Economics of Intergenerational Relationships," in Ethel Shanas and Gordon Strieb, eds., *Social Structures and the Family: Generational Relations* (Englewood Cliffs, N.J.: Prentice-Hall, 1965), pp. 267–288.

remaining issue has to do with the amount of transfer, i.e., the extent of the smoothing-out process.

In explaining the development of a scheme of retirement benefits, the role played by economic ideology cannot be overlooked, even though its quantitative importance is difficult to assess. For whatever reason, reluctance to apportion larger percentages of the nation's income to retired persons in this country—in contrast to the allocation made from much lower incomes in the Federal Republic of Germany, for example—results in a marked difference between the income of the worker and that of the retiree, even when the savings and part-time earnings of the latter are included. The problem of income maintenance in old age is magnified now by technological developments that render obsolete the job capacities of older men of low educational levels, and by the present shape of our demographic profile.

THE TEMPORAL DISTRIBUTION OF INCOME AND LEISURE

To the extent that free time is chosen by the individual in lieu of income, the worker maximizes his satisfactions, given the overall time constraint.[5] There are, however, instances in which time is not convertible into income, although such a conversion would greatly increase total utility. Unemployment is the prime example, but involuntary retirement may result in much the same removal of the income alternative. Free time in fact may have no utility in periods when it is excessive, nor work any disutility when it is very scarce.

The concept of diminishing marginal utility, whatever its shortcomings, is applicable to the consumption of leisure time as well as to the consumption of goods. It is a balancing of goods (i.e., income) and leisure that maximizes satisfactions, and this balance may be disturbed by too much free time in one stage of life and too little in another. Similarly, a somewhat more even distribution of income throughout the lifespan might increase the total utility derived from any given amount of lifetime earnings. Such a smoothing of income can be and often is accomplished by individual saving arrangements; many people, on the other hand, have extremely high time preferences for goods and relatively little willpower for saving. Reliance on some form of forced savings is therefore quite common.

5. See Lowell E. Gallaway, "The Aged and the Extent of Poverty in the United States," *Southern Economic Journal*, 33 (October, 1966), 212–222.

Since it is not possible to save the goods one produces this year for consumption several decades hence, today's worker can only acquire deferred claims against the goods produced later in the form of an annuity or "rights" to retirement benefits. In the case of an annuity, he knows how many dollars of income he will receive (though he does not know what their purchasing power will be); rights to retirement benefits, however, are not guaranteed in amount. He knows only that if payroll taxes go up now he will have fewer present dollars, retirees will have more dollars, and since benefits have never been reduced his own benefits will probably be at least as high as those which present beneficiaries are receiving, and presumably will also reflect subsequent increases in earnings levels.

The smoothing of lifetime earnings through the life cycle is more easily accomplished the longer the worklife. Hence, if leisure accrues during worklife, rather than being bunched in retirement, income-maintenance problems are less severe. The more concentrated the working time, on the other hand, the more concentrated in time are total earnings. If retirement age is lowered, the volume of income transferred from workers to nonworkers must be increased just in order to hold benefits to their present level. Attempts to set percentage limits on the payroll tax—if this is to continue to be the sole source of revenue for benefits—must therefore take account of the temporal distribution of leisure.

At present, some of our most vexing income-maintenance questions pertain to the issue of early retirement—its financing, and the extent to which the retirement years are to absorb the leisure component of the nation's economic growth. In the concentration on the financial problems of retirement, the question of the leisure's value to retirees has received little attention. It is clear, however, that any significant trend in the direction of early retirement calls for reexamination of the income-maintenance rules for at least two reasons: one, the retirement benefits available to early retirees are particularly low, and private pension coverage, though growing, is still limited to a small proportion of the total labor force; and two, the added length of the retirement period spreads thin the annual income from savings and other assets meant to be spread over the nonworking period.

Whether additional leisure in the form of early retirement is the most desired allocation of any new free time we choose to take is also a question for consideration. Although the European nations, with somewhat lower incomes and less free time, do not face this question immediately, it is evident that reduction in retirement age has a very low priority in their range of leisure preferences, which are for shorter workweeks, additional holidays in some cases, and extended education and training periods. These might well be preferred by workers in this country, if they were, in fact, alternative options. Preferences for a shorter workyear might be expressed even among those workers whose retirement incomes are adequate; certainly this would be true for persons retiring on reduced social security benefits alone.

III. THE TEMPORAL ALLOCATION OF INCOME

8. INCOME BY AGE AND OCCUPATION *

In recent studies of low-income families, much use has been made of cross-sectional data; the numbers and characteristics of families with incomes below a specified level are repeatedly cited. By contrast, analysis of the variation in the annual income of a particular family as it moved through the life cycle is meager, limited by lack of data and by the time and expense involved in longitudinal research. Information on variations in the family's needs at different stages is similarly scant. Yet the central question involved in one of our major transfers of income—the social security benefit—has to do with the extent to which we wish to smooth the income between age groups by raising benefits for retired families via taxes on the young and the middle-aged.

In general, average earnings of different age cohorts observe the same pattern in most occupations. Immediately after entry into the labor force annual earnings are low; higher incomes then accrue to each successive cohort until peak earnings are realized by the age group 45–54. The 55–64-year-old workers, the oldest full-time participants in the labor force, have incomes significantly lower than the preceding age group. Retirement income is typically less than a third of peak annual earnings. Variations in family needs, however measured, are dependent primarily on family size and age composition, and there is no necessary correlation between these needs and earnings, at different stages of the family cycle.

At first glance, differences between income and family needs at various stages of the life cycle would seem to be revealed by an examination of the income and expenditure data for different occu-

* See footnote 1, chapter 1.

pations at different ages of the family head; these figures show the excess of income over spending (or vice versa) in each stage. But since this excess or deficit is estimated from cross-sectional data, it does not reveal the financial picture of any particular family as it progresses through worklife. To show a typical family's income-expenditure relationship through time, it is necessary to project earnings through the worklife span—taking into account the increase owing to experience and seniority as well as the rise attributable to economic growth—and to estimate the increase in expenditures that may be expected to accompany the increase in income. Such a projection of the income and spending patterns of families through their working years provides some estimate of the discretionary range of income available either for financing higher consumption during worklife or for transferring additional income claims to retirees.

INCOME PATTERNS AT DIFFERENT AGES [1]

Estimates of the 1960–1961 average annual money incomes (after taxes) in six occupations are shown in Table 8.1. These incomes are

Table 8.1. Average annual money income, after taxes, by age and occupation, 1960–1961

Age	Self-employed	Profes-sional	Clerical	Skilled	Semi-skilled	Unskilled
Under 25	$4,528	$ 4,990	$4,459	$4,676	$4,602	$3,246
25–34	7,645	7,240	5,704	5,993	5,351	4,495
35–44	9,466	9,159	6,675	6,993	6,042	4,882
45–54	9,429	10,722	6,804	7,232	6,136	4,521
55–64	8,100	9,156	5,851	6,730	5,760	4,180

Source: Bureau of Labor Statistics, *Survey of Consumer Expenditures: Consumer Expenditures and Income, Urban United States*, Report 237–238, supplement 2, part A, pp. 30–34.

1. Although age-related income data are available from census reports, family expenditure data by occupation and age of family head may be drawn only from the *Survey of Consumer Expenditures* conducted by the Bureau of Labor Statistics. Because of the need for consumer expenditure patterns at different stages of the family cycle, the BLS data are used for the discussion immediately following. However, it should be noted that the BLS survey data are based on a restricted sample, which does not attempt to give adequate representation to the population of smaller cities or rural areas, or to upper-income professionals. Estimates of lifetime earnings, which were recently published by the Bureau of the Census, are discussed later in the chapter.

primarily earnings; income derived from rents, interest, dividends, etc., averages about 5 percent of total money income.[2]

The different occupations display similar patterns of income at various ages, as Figure 8.1 reveals; in all occupations initial incomes,

Figure 8.1. Annual income and expenditures by occupation and age

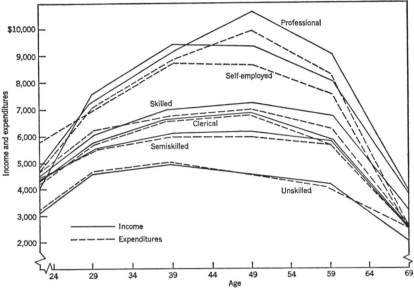

Source: See Tables 8.1 and 9.1.

the annual changes in income, and maximum annual earnings, while varying in absolute amounts, are almost identical in structure.[3]

Consider, for example, the income-age pattern in two of the occupations. *Professionals* under the age of 25 receive an average of

2. This calculation is based on money income before taxes, for all urban families and single consumers. Data on earnings as a proportion of income, by age and occupation, are not available. In addition to these major sources—earnings and the ownership of assets—public and private transfers (pensions, welfare payments, unemployment insurance), military allotments, gifts of cash, etc., constitute about 9 percent of money income before taxes. Bureau of Labor Statistics, *Survey of Consumer Expenditures: Consumer Expenditures and Income*, Urban United States, Report 237-238, supplement 3, part A, p. 12.

3. Earnings from work are based on the average annual number of labor force participants per family, which differs by occupation. For the self-employed the average is 0.98; for professionals the average is 1.06; for clerical and skilled, 1.02; for semiskilled, 0.96; for unskilled, 0.80. Ibid., pp. 30-34.

$4,990 per year after taxes. During the age span 25–34 the average is much higher: $7,240. The age group 35–44 again has higher incomes; [4] from an average of $9,159 for the 35–44 age group, earnings rise to a maximum of $10,722 during ages 45–54. Average incomes are significantly lower ($9,156) for those persons in the 55–64 age group—the group of men in their last full decade of work. For *clerical* employees under age 25 the average income is $4,459. This occupation, too, sees its fastest income growth (to $5,704) in the 25–34 age span, although the annual growth in income is only about 2.5 percent as compared with the 5.5 percent for professionals. There are further increases to $6,675 in the 35–44 and $6,804 in the 45–54 age ranges. The very small rise in the latter period is followed by a decline of almost $1,000 per year for the group in the last ten years of working life. Roughly the same pattern holds for skilled and semiskilled workers. In the case of the unskilled worker, highest earnings are received by the 35–44 age group; this is also true of the self-employed, although the average income is only slightly higher than in the subsequent age group.

The percentage rise in incomes of the self-employed and the professionals is more than twice the proportionate increase for other occupations. Peak annual earnings for professionals are 115 percent above initial earnings; for self-employed persons, the peak is 109 percent over starting incomes. For the other occupations, the increases over initial incomes are: skilled, 55 percent; clerical, 53 percent; unskilled, 50 percent; semiskilled, 33 percent. For all occupations, the highest rate of increase in average annual earnings occurs between the initial and the second stage of the work cycle.

THE IMPACT OF GROWTH ON EARNINGS

Data on the incomes by age and occupation illuminate some facets of the poverty question that have been discussed during the past half a decade. It is important to note, for example, that although relatively low incomes accrue to the youngest group in the labor force, the incomes going to the next two age groups are substantially increased in all occupations. Incomes of those persons in the last sev-

4. Earnings for college-trained personnel rise particularly rapidly between the ages of 25 and 44. See Dorothy S. Brady, *Age and Income Distribution*, United States Department of Health, Education, and Welfare, Social Security Administration, 1965, p. 33.

eral years of worklife are also noteworthy. During this period financial preparations for retirement are normally made. However, since incomes of this age cohort are lower than those of the preceding groups, there may be some tendency for 55–64-year-olds to maintain levels of living higher than can be afforded, given the need for concentrated saving for the retirement period. As subsequent review will show, the volume of expenditures at all age levels is dependent primarily on income available. Increases in disposable income accruing during worklife are likely therefore to be accompanied by higher levels of living during worklife, rather than increased saving for old age.

Cross-sectional data, however, do not shed any light on the probable income-expenditure patterns of today's labor force entrant, nor do they provide an adequate basis for estimating his capacity for accumulating income for old age. In the course of his worklife, income at the various age levels will be rising in some rough accord with overall economic growth.[5] By the same token, today's retiree did not receive the incomes during his worklife that the cross-sectional picture indicates. If he came up through the ranks of his occupation, his income at each stage was lower than the income now being paid; growth has raised the earnings of each of the occupational levels. The income problems of many of the present retirees can be explained by reference to their relatively low earnings in an earlier, less productive economic era.

GROWTH AND EARNINGS THROUGH THE WORKLIFE

Until longitudinal study affords data on lifetime earnings and consumption patterns of individual families, one may direct attention to the income of the future aged by making some assumptions regarding the earnings of today's labor force participant as he moves through the worklife cycle, and combining these projected lifetime earnings with probable expenditure patterns. On earnings, earlier work by Herman P. Miller may serve as a guide to the kinds of changes occurring

5. H. S. Houthakker has observed that "every individual may expect an upward trend in his own earnings superimposed on the cross-sectional pattern for a given year." See his "Education and Income," *Review of Economic Statistics*, 41 (February, 1959), p. 27. This growth factor is taken into account by Herman Miller in his estimates of lifetime earnings, which are indicated in the section below. See the work by Miller and Richard A. Harnseth, *Present Value of Estimated Lifetime Earnings* (Washington: Bureau of the Census, 1967).

Table 8.2. Components of change in mean income for selected cohorts of males, 1949 and 1959, United States

	Annual rate of increase in income (*percentage*)								
Years of education	Between ages 25–34 and ages 35–44			Between ages 35–44 and ages 45–54			Between ages 45–54 and ages 55–64		
	Total	Experience	Growth	Total	Experience	Growth	Total	Experience	Growth
Less than 8 years	5.5	1.8	3.7	3.3	0.8	2.5	1.9	−0.6	2.5
8 years	5.3	1.9	3.4	3.3	0.7	2.6	1.8	−0.7	2.5
1–3 years high school	5.9	2.1	3.8	3.7	0.9	2.8	2.4	−0.6	3.0
4 years high school	6.3	2.4	3.9	3.8	1.7	2.1	1.8	−0.3	2.1
1–3 years college	9.1	4.6	4.5	4.4	1.4	3.0	2.9	−0.9	3.8
4+ years college	12.7	7.6	5.1	3.5	1.5	2.0	1.2	−0.6	1.8

Source: Herman P. Miller, "Lifetime Income and Economic Growth," *American Economic Review*, 55 (September, 1965), 842–843.

through worklife.[6] Table 8.2 reproduces his estimates of the changes in mean income between ages 30 and 40, 40 and 50, and 50 and 60. Between 1949 and 1959, for example, he finds an annual increase of 12.7 percent in the income of the college graduate who moves from age 30 to age 40, an annual increase of 3.5 percent for the graduate who moves from 40 to 50, and a 1.2 percent increase for the one who goes from 50 to 60 years of age.

Miller's estimates are relevant for two reasons. First, it is clear that the annual rise in income is much greater during the male's thirties than during subsequent decades. Moreover, the difference between income growth in the thirties and the forties is especially marked for the college graduate. Second, the components of the income rise are of some importance to discussions of the aging process. Distinguishing between that portion of the increase attributable to the worker's added experience [7] and that portion due to economic growth, the author finds that the relative significance of the two sources shifts through the decades. For college graduates, experience accounts for a yearly income increase of 7.6 percent in the male's 30-to-40 age span, while growth brings another 5.1 percent. In the 40-to-50 decade, however, experience gives rise to a 1.5 percent annual increase in income, and growth assumes the larger proportion of 2.0 percent. Finally, experience has a negative impact on income during the male's fifties, and this holds for college graduates as well as for the workers with less education; except for the growth component, all incomes would drop during the last decade of work.

Increases in income during worklife are perhaps best viewed by classifying workers on the basis of educational level, rather than occupational category.[8] However, to give a rough income estimate for each of the occupations used in the earlier cross-sectional analysis, assume that persons with 4 or more years of college enter the professions; [9]

6. "Lifetime Income and Economic Growth," *American Economic Review,* 55 (September, 1965), 834–844.

7. The difference between the mean income of a cohort and that of the cohort just preceding it (as of 1949) was assumed to be attributable to experience. The remainder of the income increase of the younger cohort as it moved from 1949 to 1959 was imputed to economic growth.

8. See James N. Morgan's review of Herman P. Miller's *Income Distribution in the United States* (Washington: Bureau of the Census, 1966), in *American Economic Review,* 57 (June, 1967), 626.

9. It is interesting to note that the proportion of college-trained persons is increasing relative to those without college training, yet there is no indication that this relative increase has reduced the return on a college education. See Brady, *Age and Income Distribution,* p. 4; Herman P. Miller, "Annual and Lifetime Income in Relation to Education," *American Economic Review,* 50 (December, 1960), 962–986, and *Income Distribution in the United States,* p. 163.

those with 1–3 years of college are the self-employed; persons with high school diplomas become clerical workers; persons with 1–3 years of high school are the skilled; those with 8 years of education the semiskilled; and persons with fewer than 8 years of school the unskilled workers. Suppose further that the 1949–1959 trend in incomes continues; that economic growth raises income per year at the same rate during the male's twenties as during his thirties; that the average age of entry for persons entering professions is 22, rather than the 20 assumed for other occupations.

Under these assumptions, it is possible to illustrate the combined effects of economic growth and experience on worklife income. In the professional income profile shown earlier in Table 8.1, for example,

Table 8.3. Estimated average annual incomes through worklife, with economic growth component included for workers aged 25 and under in 1960–1961

Age	Self-employed	Profes-sional	Clerical	Skilled	Semi-skilled	Unskilled
Under 25	$ 4,528	$ 4,990	$ 4,459	$ 4,676	$ 4,602	$ 3,246
25–34	10,149	9,681	7,785	8,111	7,179	5,918
35–44	17,582	17,845	12,388	12,784	10,722	8,899
45–54	23,591	23,316	15,385	17,106	13,956	11,031
55–64	32,946	26,322	17,994	22,487	17,489	13,780

Source: Income data for workers under 25 taken from *Consumer Expenditures and Income*, BLS Report 237–238, tables 15a–15e. Incomes for 25–34 and succeeding cohorts calculated by compounding the growth rates indicated in table 15, and adding the 1960–1961 differences in incomes of age cohorts (table 8.1).

the 1960–1961 BLS data show an average annual income after taxes of approximately $4,990 for the youngest age group and $7,240 for the 25–34 cohort. To this difference of $2,250, attributable to whatever experience, maturity, skill, etc., the older group has acquired, must be added a growth factor of 5.1 percent per year for 8 years, giving an average annual income of $9,681 for the 30-year-old male.[10] During the next decade growth again adds 5.1 percent per annum, which, when added to the experience differential of $2,919, raises the average income of the 40-year-old to $17,845 (Table 8.3).

Both growth and experience add noticeably less to income for the 45–54-year-olds. The annual growth component is 2.0 percent, which raises average annual income (when the experience factor is added) to $23,316 for the man aged 50. Since the experience factor is negative

10. Estimates of the contribution of economic growth are taken from Miller, "Lifetime Income and Economic Growth." Cross-sectional differences ($2,250 in this instance), assumed to be due to experience, are taken from table 8.2.

between 55 and 64, the effect of growth is only to offset this tendency and raise income slightly. By the time the workers reach retirement age, earnings average $26,322 per year.

Similar computations yield the estimated incomes at various ages for the different occupations. At the time of retirement for most workers, average incomes will be quite high by today's standards, once the impact of economic growth is taken into account (see Figure 8.2). Other growth assumptions could be made, yielding different future incomes for the various occupations; the assumption of no growth factor is, however, clearly invalid.

Figure 8.2. Income and expenditures by occupation and age, 1960–1961, and projected worklife income (professional)

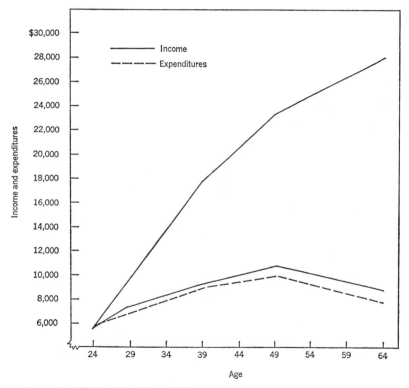

Source: See Tables 8.1, 8.3, and 9.1.

9. ANNUAL EXPENDITURES DURING WORKLIFE

Expectation of a higher income in the future offers a strong inducement to spend heavily during the present, and the ease with which Americans can borrow against future earnings further weakens any resistance to exceed current income. Since incomes vary even during worklife and suffer great extremes before and after the working years, and since family needs, which differ also at different stages of the life cycle, are not correlated with income variations, attempts to hold current expenditures to current income are not necessarily advisable. Thus young families tend to borrow heavily for the purchase of housing and durables, while families with heads in their forties frequently borrow for the college expenses of their children.

The reapportionment of a family's lifetime income in accordance with its needs is accomplished in large measure through the use of consumer credit. Given a high rate of time preference for goods, however, the tendency for many families is to reallocate income quite generously to the present, giving much less attention to the low-income retirement period. The difficulties of accumulating sufficient private savings to maintain during retirement the levels of consumption achieved during the worklife, particularly during periods of rapid economic growth, are analyzed in a later chapter. In the review immediately following, 1960–1961 average family expenditures, by occupation and age of family head, are compared with average incomes in the respective categories. The question of the behavior of expenditures through the working portion of the family cycle is then posed, in order to focus attention on the possible impact of growth on future consumption-savings patterns, and to examine the effect on retirement incomes of a temporal reapportionment of consumption.

EXPENDITURES AT DIFFERENT AGES

Data reported in the *Survey of Consumer Expenditures* provide a rough picture of the consumption levels observed by the families headed by persons of different occupations and ages. Although the level of expenditures is admittedly constrained by income, age-related differences in income are not always paralleled by comparable differences in spending.[1] In all occupations, income exceeds expenditures during some stage of the family's life cycle, and conversely, expenditures are greater at some stages for all occupational groups.

Expenditures[2] at different ages of the family head are shown in Table 9.1. Taking the clerical worker as an example, the data indicate

Table 9.1. Average annual expenditures, by age and occupation, 1960–1961

Age	Self-employed	Profes-sional	Clerical	Skilled	Semi-skilled	Unskilled
Under 25	$5,912	$5,088	$4,526	$4,814	$4,544	$3,469
25–34	6,905	6,941	5,632	6,144	5,367	4,599
35–44	8,701	8,795	6,668	6,733	5,947	5,051
45–54	8,694	9,933	6,815	6,945	5,971	4,540
55–64	7,639	8,281	5,672	6,251	5,629	4,064

Source: Consumer Expenditures and Income, BLS Report no. 237–238, pp. 30–34.

that spending averages $4,526 for the family whose head is under 25 years of age, $5,632 for the family in the 25–34 age bracket, $6,668 for the 35–44, $6,815 for the 45–54, and $5,672 for the 55–64 cohort. Expenditures in the family headed by the 25–34-year-old are thus about one-fourth again as high as the level for the preceding cohort; for the 35–44 age group consumption is higher still, by about one-fifth. Families with heads aged 45–54 spend only slightly more than the preceding age group, while average expenditures by the families of the

1. See Sidney Goldstein, *Consumption Patterns of the Aged* (Philadelphia: University of Pennsylvania Press, 1960).
2. Expenditures are calculated as after-tax income, less the net change in assets. Thus, if after-tax income is $5,000 and the net change in assets is +$100, expenditures are taken as $4,900. On the other hand, if after-tax income is $5,000 and net change in assets is −$100, then expenditures are taken as $5,100. Expenditures include current consumption plus outlays for durables.

55–64-year-olds are about one-sixth lower than the level maintained by the 45–54 age group.[3]

INCOME-EXPENDITURE DIFFERENCES BY AGE AND OCCUPATION

The relation between income and expenditures for families at different stages of the life cycle is depicted in Figure 9.1.

Self-employed and *professional* workers' incomes are well above ex-

Figure 9.1. Income and expenditures by occupation and age, 1960–1961

Source: See Figure 8.1.

3. There is some evidence that surveys such as the Bureau of Labor Statistics *Consumer Expenditures and Income* understate income and overstate expenditures. See Irwin Friend and Stanley Schor, "Who Saves?" *Review of Economics and Statistics,* 41 (May, 1959), 221, and Bureau of Labor Statistics, *Consumer Expenditures and Income,* pp. 6, 9.

penditures for practically all age groups, as might easily have been predicted. Except for the early stages of worklife, after-tax incomes afford a wide margin for higher current consumption levels, or for savings and the purchase of future income claims. The amount of the excess of income over expenditures during a lifetime cannot of course be estimated from the cross-sectional data—the family head aged 55–64 did not have in his younger working years the income now accruing to younger cohorts. However, it is clear that a perpetuation of the current incomes going to the different age groups would result in lifetime earnings sufficient to guarantee today's self-employed and professional employee substantial discretionary margins.

Clerical workers' earnings and expenditures are closely balanced for all age groups. In contrast to the margins available to self-employed and professional workers, the clerical worker, should he receive the average income accruing at the different ages, would have a net saving of only about $3,300 (charging dissaving a 6 percent rate of interest and paying saving a 5 percent rate) by the time he reached retirement at age 65. For persons in this occupation, substantial saving for old age is thus possible only if consumption levels are reduced, or if incomes rise in the course of the coming decades.

Among *skilled* and *semiskilled* workers, spending exceeds income during the early labor force years; income is high enough to match the expenditure level only for those workers aged 35 and over. Cohorts aged 45–54 have incomes in excess of expenditures, some margin persisting through age 64. Although semiskilled employees earn less than skilled workers during their working years, expenditures also absorb proportionately less of their after-tax income. As a result, the semiskilled worker who received the present average income accruing at the different ages would have a worklife balance of about $7,300, as compared with the skilled worker's $3,800.

Unskilled workers do not receive enough income to cover their expenditures at any age except the 55–64 span, and even then there is no significant income margin. As in the case of the clerical workers, no saving appears possible unless the expenditures are cut substantially, or money incomes rise. Moreover, it is evident that this occupational group requires transfers of income, not only in the retirement years, but through most of worklife as well.

In summary, annual incomes exceed expenditures of the self-employed and professional workers' families for most of the age cohorts, leaving sources of savings at practically all stages of worklife. Semiskilled workers, whose expenditures are held below income during the middle and later years, also have a small margin for saving. Clerical and skilled workers barely balance expenditures with income in total, with the years of slight deficits roughly offset by years of small savings. In the case of unskilled workers, no balance of income with expenditure is achieved except very briefly in the 55–64 age period.

INCOME GROWTH AND EXPENDITURES

The 1960–1961 data on income and expenditures at different ages give a rough indication of the extent to which income constrained spending in that year. Figure 9.1 shows the close correlation of expenditures with current after-tax incomes for families in most of the age groups for most of the occupations. In order to gauge the income potential for the retirement period, however, it is necessary to determine the probable pattern of consumer expenditure through the lifespan, given the much higher real incomes that are likely to be forthcoming. How will the families' consumption patterns be affected by the rise in incomes that will accompany continued economic growth? More specifically, what portion of the higher incomes will be preempted for consumption during worklife and what portion will be available for savings or transfers?

If economic growth should raise future incomes well above present expenditure levels, and if levels of living were to remain fixed through even a decade of such growth, the greater margin of income over consumption would make possible expanded investment (including investment in the education of the young) or increased consumption by other groups (for example, retirees). The supposition that workers' expenditures will remain at something close to their present level is unwarranted, however, on the basis of past experience; nor would such a freezing of living levels be necessarily desirable.

Perhaps the most reasonable assumption as to future consumption expenditures is to suppose that their increase will be proportional to the rise in income. Goldsmith found that the personal rate of saving "failed to show a marked upward or downward trend during the past half century." [4] Modigliani and Brumberg have hypothesized a constant saving-income ratio.[5] They argue that households wish to main-

4. Raymond W. Goldsmith, *A Study of Saving in the United States*, vol. 1, National Bureau of Economic Research (Princeton, N.J.: Princeton University Press, 1955), p. 7.

5. Franco Modigliani and Richard Brumberg, "Utility Analysis and the Consumption Function: An Interpretation of Cross-Sectional Data," in Kenneth K. Kurihara, *Post-Keynesian Economics* (New Brunswick, N.J.: Rutgers University Press, 1954), p. 430.

tain a certain level of saving to provide for emergencies, retirement, etc. Thus, a 10 percent increase in income would be matched by a 10 percent rise in expenditures.[6] Any departure from this proportion is due to short-term or unanticipated fluctuations in income and is not typical of the usual relationship between income and expenditures.[7]

If consumer expenditures continue to absorb the proportions of income used for that purpose in 1960–1961, the bulk of the gradually rising incomes of labor force participants will be absorbed by their rising consumption, but the residual will nevertheless be significant for men in many occupations. For the professional and self-employed persons, the worklife totals would of course be quite high; skilled and semiskilled would also have substantial balances, and the clerical workers somewhat less. Since expenditures exceed income for the unskilled workers at most ages, a portion of the projected rise in incomes would need to be used to equate expenditures and income. Some net saving could result in the last ten years of worklife, should the projected expenditures-income ratio be the same as that observed in the cross-sectional data.

If the projected rise in earnings should be accompanied by a willingness to save for the retirement years, a smoother distribution of income through the life cycle would of course be accomplished. Although it can be demonstrated that higher disposable income in the past has been associated with increased consumption, it can also be argued that previous generations of workers have not had sufficiently high or stable incomes to permit lifetime savings of any magnitude. A continuation of recent rates of growth, plus an increased awareness of retirement as a life stage, could combine to produce somewhat better financial preparation through private savings. In the two chapters immediately following, rough estimates are made of the range within which income could be smoothed during the last three decades of life by shifting consumption expenditures from work to retirement years.

6. Ibid., p. 419.
7. Ibid., p. 430. On the possible inaccuracies associated with data collected over a relatively short period, see Harold Lydall, "The Life Cycle in Income, Saving, and Asset Ownership," *Econometrica*, 23 (April, 1955), 145, and Ralph B. Bristol, "Factors Associated with Income Variability," *American Economic Review*, 48 (May, 1958), 279–280.

10. REAPPORTIONING CONSUMPTION AFTER AGE 50: A MODEL *

A reallocation of expenditures from the working to the retirement period would probably not have solved the financial hardships confronting the present aged, most of whose lifetime earnings were extremely low by today's standards, and many of whose working careers were interrupted by unemployment during the acute depression of the 1930s. For workers now in the labor force, however, the possibility of achieving any target level of consumption during retirement, through a reduction in worklife consumption outlays, needs to be considered. The questions can be posed in the following manner: To what extent would systematic savings during worklife serve to offset the sharp drop in income normally accompanying retirement from the labor force? What volume of private savings is required (in addition to social security benefits) to guarantee during retirement the level of living achieved at age 65? At age 50? Can a family with earnings at, say, the median level realistically hope to accumulate savings in the necessary amount?

In the ensuing analysis, we are concerned primarily with the extent to which a family can approximate a target level of retirement consumption (by assumption, the level achieved when the household head is age 50) by increasing personal savings during the latter part of worklife. Specifically, we shall first examine the impact of a savings scheme inaugurated at age 50, under which all subsequent increases in income are saved for retirement, then prorated over the retirement

* The author wishes to acknowledge the assistance of Professor Sydney H. High in the preparation of chaps. 10 and 11.

period. Under simplifying assumptions as to retirement age and age at death, social security benefits, and the value of home owned, it is then possible to indicate what proportion of age-50 consumption (and age-65 consumption) can be maintained in retirement. Second, we suppose that the savings plan involves the setting aside of one-half the increments to income during the last 15 years of worklife. Finally, the assumption is made that families continue to save in approximately the pattern they now observe.

In each of the three cases, the retirement consumption level as a proportion of consumption at the preretirement ages, 50 and 65, is shown. These proportions afford an approximation of the role private savings could play in the solution of the retirement-income drop, given various propensities to consume during the latter part of worklife. Increasing the length of the retirement-planning period by beginning to save for retirement at a younger age, or extending worklife beyond age 65, or increasing the amount of the assumed social security benefit, or assuming the ownership of a private pension, paid for by the employer, would increase the proportion of preretirement consumption attainable. In this preliminary version of the model, none of these changes have been made. We have, however, drawn some tentative conclusions regarding the size of the income gap (given the targeted level of retirement consumption), the dollar value of end-of-worklife income necessary to achieve target consumption, and the growth rate necessary, in turn, to raise income to that level by age 65.

MODELS OF THE TIME ALLOCATION OF CONSUMPTION

High incomes during worklife do not necessarily dictate high consumption during that period; one can save for retirement, thereby smoothing consumption in accordance with the family's preferences. Although attempts to save sufficient funds to maintain during retirement the consumption levels observed during worklife are often doomed to failure in a period when real incomes are rising,[1] there is obviously the option of postponing some consumption during high-income years in return for additional (presumably higher-utility) consumption in the later period.

1. See Juanita M. Kreps and John O. Blackburn, "The Impact of Economic Growth on Retirement Incomes," *Hearings before the Special Committee on Aging,* United States Senate, 90th Congress, 1st session, 1967, pp. 58–64.

Allocation of Consumption during the Lifetime

Extending the analysis of consumption and saving presented by
Modigliani and Brumberg,[2] and by Friedman,[3] Arena has shown the
effect of allocating consumption equally over a planning period, in
this instance an economic lifetime.[4] In brief, he shows first, the case in
which the smoothed consumption absorbs all earnings, with initial
wealth and final wealth being zero; second, the effect on consumption
of a windfall capital gain, all of which is allocated evenly during the
remainder of the lifetime; third, the effect of a permanent rise in income (which again raises consumption during the remaining years) ;
and finally, the instance in which consumption throughout life is held
to the rate necessary to provide a target bequest.

Arena's first model, assuming no initial or final target wealth, is
shown by his diagram (Figure 10.1), depicting consumption (*C*)

Figure 10.1. Allocation of consumption over the life cycle

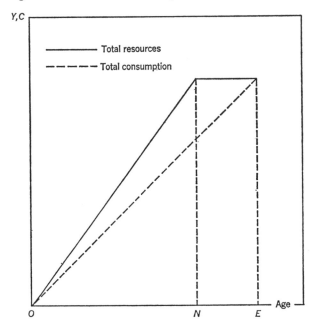

Source: J. J. Arena, "The Wealth Effect and Consumption:
A Statistical Inquiry," *Yale Economic Essays*, 3 (1963), 257.

2. Modigliani and Brumberg, "Utility Analysis and the Consumption Function,"
pp. 388–436.
3. Friedman, *A Theory of the Consumption Function.*
4. John J. Arena, "The Wealth Effect and Consumption: A Statistical Inquiry,"
Yale Economic Essays, 3 (Fall, 1963) , 251–303.

that is smoothed throughout the lifespan. The consumer earns income
(*Y*) until time *N*, when he retires. During the retirement period, *NE*,
he dissaves. He dies at *E*, having consumed his lifetime income, no
more and no less. The author stresses his assumptions in these and his
other models: the interest rate is zero; pure time preference exists,
annual income is constant throughout worklife, and exact lifespan is
known.

For a variation on the notion of smoothing consumption through
the lifespan, as depicted by Arena, we shall assume here that preparation for retirement begins at age 50, and that the planning period
covers only the last 30 years of life—that is, the 15 years of remaining
worklife and 15 years in retirement.[5] On the further assumption that
assets acquired prior to the planning period are in the form of home
ownership,[6] the task is then to allocate total income received (earnings for 15 years, plus interest on the savings, which begin to accumulate at age 51; retirement benefits; prorated value of the home,
starting at age 65) over the remaining lifespan.

Any one of several assumptions can be made regarding the degree
of income smoothing: one, that the consumption level at age 50 be
held constant, allowing the increases in income thereafter to cumulate
for retirement period; two, that half the income increments be consumed with the other half being applied to retirement income; or
three, that some other proportion of the increase in income be saved.
Alternatively, we can pose the question: What reduction (if any) in
age-50 consumption is required to permit equal annual consumption
throughout the planning period?

Allocation of Consumption during the Last 30 Years of Life

In contrast to previous models treating lifetime allocation of income and consumption, we are concerned here with the "preretirement" (age 50–64) and retirement years (age 65–79). Although a reordering of consumption for purposes of accumulating retirement

5. Saving for retirement on the part of low- and moderate-income families is
unlikely to begin until children have become self-supporting. For this reason, age
50 is selected as the beginning of the planning period; age 45, or even 40, may in
some instances be the appropriate age.

6. See Board of Governors, "Size and Composition of Consumer Saving," *Federal
Reserve Bulletin*, 53 (January, 1967), 32–50. Data on the composition of saving, by
age group, show that in the youngest group of consumer units (those with heads
under 35) there were few large savers or dissavers. Increases in equities in homes
and automobiles accounted for about three-fourths of the group's total saving.
Larger savings occurred in the 45–54 age group; even for this group, however,
increases in home and automobile equities constituted 57 percent of savings, with
all liquid assets amounting to one-fourth ($450) of the total. See table 2, p. 45.

income may thus occur in this model only at age 50, an earlier or later age can equally well be chosen; in fact, one purpose of the analysis is to identify the age at which consumption-savings patterns must be altered, if retirement consumption is to be held at the desired proportion of preretirement consumption. Moreover, the assumption that the planning period begins at age 50 does not preclude the accumulation of fixed assets, notably the home, the value of which is decumulated during retirement. Nor does it rule out the acquisition of claims for the retirement benefits that constitute the major proportion of retirement income. In essence, then, the shortened planning period merely restricts to 15 the number of years in which the marginal propensity to consume—that is, the proportion of the increases in disposable income spent for consumption—can be reduced, in order to permit an increase in total annual consumption during the last 15 years of life.

The model makes the following assumptions.[7]

1. The decision-making unit is the family; in some cases the "family" is a single individual.

2. There is a linear increase in income [8] until age R, at which time retirement occurs. Accordingly, we can write preretirement income as

$$(1) \qquad Y_a = Y_{a-1} + k,$$

where $k =$ the constant annual increase in income, $Y =$ income, and subscripts refer to age.

For realism, we shall assume that the rate of increase in income after age P [9] is less than the rate of increase in income before age P.[10] In that case we can specify the preplanning preretirement income as

$$(2) \qquad Y_{t'} = Y_{t'-1} + l,$$

where $t' = w, \ldots, P - 1$, w is the beginning year of working life and $l =$ the constant annual increase in income prior to age R. Moreover, the postplanning, preretirement income can be written similarly as

$$(3) \qquad Y_{P+t} = Y_{(P+t)-1} + m,$$

7. The model is presented in three ways: mathematically, geometrically, and verbally. Those so disposed may skip the mathematics and proceed to the remainder with no loss of continuity.

8. It will become evident that the assumption of linear increases in income can readily be dropped in favor of nonlinear increases, with no effect on the analytical results of the model.

9. P is the year at which planning and saving for retirement begins. This is assumed to be 50 years of age.

10. The assumed change in the rate of increases in income is in accordance with changes indicated in Miller, "Lifetime Income and Economic Growth," pp. 842–843.

where $t =$ the number of years which have lapsed since the initiation of the planning period, and $m =$ the constant annual increase in income after age P.

> *Note.* It will be recalled that we have assumed the increase in income after age P to be lower than the increase prior to age P; therefore, $l > m$.

3. Once working life is begun at age w, consumption is a function of current income until age P.[11] That is,

$$(4) \qquad\qquad C_{w,\dots,P} = f(Y_{w,\dots,P}),$$

and since $Y = C + S$, then

$$(5) \qquad\qquad \begin{aligned} S_{w,\dots,P} &= f(Y_{w,\dots,P}) \\ &= (Y_{w,\dots,P}) - C_{w,\dots,P}. \end{aligned}$$

4. While income continues to increase after age P and until retirement at age R, consumption does not. Rather, we shall assume that at age P the decision-making unit has reared its family and begins to plan for retirement. Accordingly, we shall assume that in planning for retirement, the family does so with the following expectations: [12] to live until age D,[13] and to have no change in total annual real consumption. The decision-making unit may undergo changes in taste and consumption patterns; it merely makes no change in its total consumption. Therefore, all increases in income after age P are saved for income maintenance during the retirement period.

We can therefore write consumption and saving in the preretirement, postplanning period as

$$(6) \qquad\qquad Y_{P+t} = Y_{P(t-1)} + m$$

$$(7) \qquad\qquad C_{(P+t)} = f(Y_P),$$

then

$$(8) \qquad\qquad \begin{aligned} S_{(P+t)} &= f(Y_{P+m}) \\ &\equiv f(Y_{P+m}). \end{aligned}$$

11. The consumption function chosen was merely for simplicity. More complicated ones (that is, logged consumption functions) could equally well have been chosen.

12. As will become evident, the particular age of planning (P), retirement (R), and death (D), are not vital to the general results of the model, although different assumptions will of course call forth varying results.

13. We shall assume the individual expects to live r years after retirement. For realism, we may take D to be 80 years of age; therefore, if $R = 65$ years, then $r = 15$ years.

Note. It follows that interest-free assets accumulated between P and R are given by

$$A_a = \int_P^R \left(Y_P + m \right) dt,$$

while assets with interest are given by the interest-rate multiple of the right-hand side of the above equation, cumulated for each year. Total assets are given by

$$A_a = A_{P-1} + \int_P^R \left(Y_P + m \right) dt.$$

Since the largest component of assets held by the aged is in a nonliquid form (see Epstein and Murray, *The Aged Population of the United States*, table 4.3, p. 312), we shall assume that all assets accumulated prior to age P are nonliquid. This assumption is hardly a crucial one, and indeed is relaxed in our test of the model (see the appendix, pp. 118–129), to incorporate the value of home equity. The assumption merely allows us to assume that all assets accumulated after age P are used for income maintenance during retirement.

5. The individual can also expect income transfers on his retirement. These transfers, that is, social security benefits, private pensions, etc., will be designated as T. We can therefore write postretirement income and consumption as

(9) $$Y_{R+r} = f \left(\sum_{t=P}^R S_t + T \right)$$

(10) $$C_{R+r} = f(Y_{R+r})$$
$$\equiv f \left(\sum_{t=P}^R S_t + T \right),$$

where $r = 0, \ldots, D - R$, or the number of years which have lapsed since retirement.

Note. It is obvious that if $C_P = f(Y_P)$ and $C_{P+t} = f(Y_P)$, as in equation 6, while $Y_{P+t} = f(Y_{P+t-1} + m)$ from equation 7, then $S_t = m$. Therefore, (Y_{R+r}) in equation 9 would become

$$Y_{(R+r)} = f \left[\left(\sum_{t=P}^r m \right) + Ta \right],$$

and (C_{R+r}) in equation 10 would become

$$C_{R+r} = f\left[\left(\sum_{t=P}^{r} m\right) + T\right].$$

Further, while we have not here incorporated any term for the interest appreciation of assets $(= \mathrm{IR})$, it is obvious we could do so as follows:

$$\Upsilon_{R+r} = f\left[(\mathit{IR})\left(\sum_{t=P}^{r} m\right) + Ta\right],$$

and therefore consumption at $(R + r)$ could be similarly increased.

Figure 10.2. Allocation of consumption after age 50

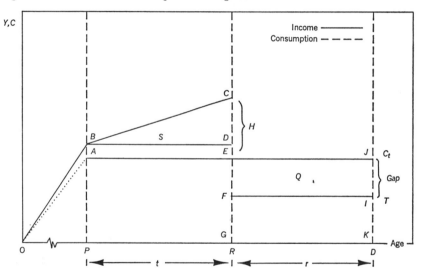

The problem of lifetime allocation of income can be depicted geometrically.

Figure 10.2 indicates that the problem facing the decision-making unit is to determine a constant level of consumption, beginning at age *P*, which will insure that the area of saving, *S* $(= ABCE)$ at least equals the difference [14] between income transfers, or *T* $(= FGHI)$ and

14. We shall call the difference between the targeted level of consumption and the income transfers the income gap or, symbolically, $C - T = Gap$.

the targeted level of consumption, or C_r $(= EGHJ)$.

The area of saving, S, is composed of the rectangle $ABDE$ plus that of a triangle BDC.[15] It is important to observe that the rectangle and the triangle share a common base $(AE = BD)$; this base represents the time period of saving for retirement income and may need to be lengthened as the area Q increases.[16] Since the base of the two areas of savings is commonly shared we can determine the total area of saving, or S, between ages P and R as follows:

$$S = A_z + A_q,$$

where

$$A_z = \text{area of rectangle,}$$

and

$$A_q = \text{area of triangle,}$$

or, from the appropriate formulas,

$$S = b_z h_z + \left(\frac{b_q h_q}{2} \right),$$

where b_z and b_q are the bases of the rectangle and the triangle, respectively, and h_z and h_q are their respective heights. Since $AE = BD$, then $b_z = b_q$; so factoring, we get

$$S = b \left(h_z + \frac{h_q}{2} \right),$$

and rewriting,

$$\frac{2S}{b} = 2h_z + h_q.$$

However, since we have assumed linear increases in income, we are interested only in the income during the last years of working life (that is, Y_R), for this gives us the height (H) of the area of saving (S). Therefore, we can write H as

$$\frac{2S}{b} = \frac{2S}{t}.$$

15. It will be recalled that we have assumed assets AOB are in the form of nonliquid assets.

16. The income gap, Gap, will increase under any or all of the following circumstances: (a) C_T increases with T and r constant; (b) r increases with C_T and T constant; (c) T decreases with C_T and r constant.

If we allow t (period of saving for income maintenance during retirement) to vary by some coefficient (x), then we can write

$$\frac{H}{x} = \frac{2S}{tx}.$$

We can illustrate the geometry with the following examples:

Example 1. Assume at age 50 the family unit determines to hold its level of consumption constant through the remaining 30 years of life. Specifically, assume a current disposable income of $7,000, of which 6/7, or $6,000, is consumed. Let retirement occur at age 65, death at age 80, and, further, let social security benefits amount to $2,500. Under these assumed conditions, what level of income at age 65 will insure sufficient savings to maintain the targeted level of consumption? That is, we have $P = 50$, $t = 15$, $D = 80$, $X = 1$, $C_r = \$6,000$, $T = \$2,500$, and $r = 15$. Then,

$$\begin{aligned}
\text{area in } Q &= (Gap) \quad (r) \\
&= (6,000 - 2,500) \quad (15) \\
&= \$52,500
\end{aligned}$$

Then, if S is to equal Q, H will have to be

$$(H)\left(\frac{1}{x}\right) = \frac{2Q}{tx},$$

or

$$H = \frac{2(52,500)}{15} = \$7,000.$$

We can write the requisite income in the last year of working life as

$$\begin{aligned}
Y_R &= H + C_T \\
&= 7,000 + 6,000 \\
Y_R &= \$13,000.
\end{aligned}$$

Example 2. On the other hand, we may wish to know whether current consumption levels are too high to be maintained throughout retirement, given the current income, the income in the last year of working life, the size of transfers during retirement, the age of retirement, and the age of death. That is, we ask whether C_T can be maintained, given values of T, R, D, r, H, Y_P and Y_R.

Let $C_T = f(Y_P)$ where $APC = 0.90$ and $Y_P = \$7,000$, such that $C_T = \$6,300$.
Further let

$$\begin{aligned}
T &= \$2,500 \\
Y_P &= \$7,000 \\
Y_R &= \$9,500.
\end{aligned}$$

Then $H = Y_R - C_T = 9,500 - 6,300$
$$H = \$3,200,$$
and since $D = 80$
$P = 50$
$R = 65,$
then $t = R - P = 65 - 50$
$t = 15$
and $r = D - R = 80 - 65$
$r = 15.$
Now $Q = (Gap)(r)$ where $Gap = C_T - T$
$= (6,300 - 2,500) \quad (15)$
$Q = \$57,000.$

From our formula for H (above) we know that, given our values of C_T and T, H must be

$$H = \frac{2Q}{t}$$
$$= \frac{2(57,000)}{15}$$
$$H = \$7,600$$

if C_T is to obtain. However, we know that the actual value of H is $Y_R - C_T = \$3,200$. Accordingly, we can write $\$3,200 = 2S/t$, where S is the amount of assets actually accumulated between P and R, and for which we must solve. Solving, we get

$$\$3,200 = \frac{2S}{15}$$
$$2S = (15)(3,200)$$
$$= 48,000$$
$$S = \$24,000.$$

In short, then, we see that at Y_R the decision-making unit will find he cannot continue consuming at his current rate during retirement, since Q exceeds S by $\$33,000$. The family must therefore either lower consumption during retirement by $\$33,000$, which if prorated equally over the remainder of life would be $\$33,000/15$, or $\$2,200$ per year, such that $C_{R,\dots,D} = C_T - \$2,200$ or $\$4,100$; or the family head must decide to work longer than R.

Note. In this case, if Y_R continues to obtain, the decision-making unit would need to work for the period $33,000/H$ or $33,000/7,600$, or $4\frac{1}{3}$ years longer than he had anticipated, in order to maintain C_T until expected death. In fact, such an option may of course not be open to him.

SUMMARY

When a family head begins at age 50 to save for retirement at age 65, he is assumed to have as given knowledge: the income he will receive each year during the remainder of worklife; annual income transfers during retirement; the age of death. With this knowledge, the family knows how much (both annually and for the remainder of the lifespan) it requires to close the gap between target consumption and income via transfers. The family can then theoretically begin saving at some rate which will insure that total assets accumulated prior to retirement will equal postretirement needs. The particular savings rate chosen will be determined by the desired age of retirement, the increments to income prior to retirement, and the target level of consumption. Should retirement income requirements exceed expected savings of the preretirement period, the family must alter one of several variables: (*a*) the age of retirement might be increased; or (*b*) the targeted level of retirement consumption might be decreased; or (*c*) the preretirement level of consumption might be lowered; or (*d*) some combination of the above might be altered.

On the other hand, should preretirement savings be expected to equal or exceed postretirement needs, the decision-making unit would foresee a savings surplus which might be used to increase consumption during retirement or be left as an estate.

We have presented a framework for the time allocation of income when the values of certain economic variables are given. Since the relevant variables are not fully known for any given family, the model lacks predictive value in individual cases. On the other hand, for large socioeconomic groups the relevant values are available; the model therefore has obvious implications for public policy. Accordingly, attention is now turned to the available data on income levels at age 50 and propensities to consume, to probable rates of income growth after age 50, and to income transfers after age 65.

11. REAPPORTONING CONSUMPTION AFTER AGE 50: EMPIRICAL RESULTS

For an investigation of the model's use in estimating possible retirement consumption levels, income data for six occupational groups are taken from the 1960–61 Bureau of Labor Statistics *Survey of Consumer Expenditures*.[1] Disposable personal income is then derived [2] for families with heads aged 50. These income figures are extrapolated to 1975 at an assumed annual rate of growth of 2 percent, yielding estimates of disposable income for families with heads aged 65 in 1975, by occupational group.

Disposable income is assumed to continue to grow from age 50 through age 64 (line *BC*, Figure 10.2) at a rate of 2 percent. From the projected disposable income at the end of worklife, we subtract disposable income at age 50—a difference identical with *H* in Figure 10.2. Consumption is derived by multiplying the disposable personal income at age 50 by the appropriate average propensity to consume.[3]

1. United States Department of Labor, Bureau of Labor Statistics, *Survey of Consumer Expenditures, 1960–61; Cross-Classification of Family Characteristics: Total United States, Urban and Rural, 1960–61,* table 15d, p. 33. Washington: Government Printing Office, 1966.
2. From table 15d, ibid. The figure, "other money receipts," is added to "money income after taxes."
3. The average propensities to consume used are:

THE CONSUMPTION VARIANTS

We may consider three income-allocation variants:

1. *The parsimonious-consumption variant* is one in which the household attempts to attain during retirement that level of consumption reached at age 50. This variant asumes that the value of β in equation 8 equals one; from age 50 through age 64, consumption remains constant and all increments to income are saved for retirement period.

2. *The practical-consumption variant* differs from the basic variant by assuming that the value of β is 0.50. One-half of all increments to income are saved and the rest are used for current consumption.

3. *The profligate-consumption variant* assumes that the value of β is identical with the average values of the average propensities to save applicable to the income classes of the occupational groups as they move from age 50 to age 65.[4]

Given the difference between income at age 64 and at age 50, we calculate the value of assets accumulated during the 15 years (or the

Occupation	APC
Total	0.91
Self-employed	0.91
Salaried	0.68
Clerical	0.91
Skilled workers	0.91
Semiskilled workers	0.96
Unskilled workers	1.00

Source: Bureau of Labor Statistics, *Study of Consumer Expenditures*, 1950, vol. 18, tables 1, 4, 5.

4. Specifically, this results in the following values of β:

Occupation	APC
Total	0.875
Self-employed	0.875
Salaried	0.680
Clerical	0.875
Skilled Workers	0.875
Semi-skilled Workers	0.900
Unskilled workers	0.980

Source: See n. 3 above.

area S) by multiplying the average annual income increments by the assumed interest rate (6 percent), and cumulating.

With targeted consumption (C_T) and transfers (T) given, we know the area Q or the amount by which the accumulated assets and interest, when prorated over the remaining lifespan, fall short of the assets required to provide target consumption for the retirement period. Alternatively, we can estimate potential annual income during the 15 years of retirement: the prorated value of the assets held at age 65, plus transfers.

Taking potential income as a percentage of targeted consumption, and as a percentage of consumption at age 65, we indicate the difference between ex post and ex ante consumption.

Thus far we have not taken into account the value of the home which was purchased before age 50. We now prorate the value of the home [5] over the retirement period in order to show the proportion of targeted consumption that could be achieved if *all* assets were used, leaving (as in Arena's first model) no bequest. The calculations and resulting values are reported in the Appendix.

CONSUMPTION LEVELS UNDER THREE VARIANTS

The calculations shown in the Appendix permit some tentative conclusions regarding the discrepancy between assets required to maintain targeted consumption during retirement and assets available at age 65; the amount by which ex post consumption must fall below ex ante consumption, given the assets available at age 65; or the volume of saving (and by implication, the income) which must obtain at age 65, if targeted consumption is to be achieved.

For the parsimonious family which saves all increments to income during the last 15 years of worklife, the estimates reveal a potential retirement income of 83 percent of targeted consumption (the level achieved at age 50), and only 67 percent of the age-65 consumption level. When home value is prorated over the retirement period, consumption in retirement rises to 94 percent of the targeted amount, or 75 percent of the level reached at age 65. The family which saves half its increases in earnings from age 50 through 64 is able to consume 62 percent of targeted consumption and 50 percent of the age-65 level; these proportions rise to 72 percent and 58 percent when home value is prorated. The family which continues to consume in accord-

5. See Epstein and Murray, *The Aged Population of the United States*, p. 71.

ance with its previous pattern can afford a consumption level of 46 percent of the targeted amount and 37 percent of the consumption at the end of worklife. When home value is prorated, consumption rises to 57 percent of the age 50, and 46 percent of the age 65 level. Rates of growth in income, total volumes of savings, etc., necessary to achieve the targeted levels of consumption are also indicated in the Appendix.

In summary, the three variants on the basic model indicate the effects of different savings decisions, made at age 50, on the levels of consumption attainable during the last 30 years of life. Once a target consumption level is specified and there are known values for income during the remainder of worklife, life expectancy, retirement benefits, and fixed assets accumulated prior to age 50, the gap between ex post and ex ante consumption can be estimated. Alternatively, the income growth rate necessary to achieve target consumption during the assumed 15 years of retirement can be derived. Or the number of working years required to achieve target consumption, given the actual growth rate, can be derived. Finally, the proportion of target consumption actually attainable during retirement, and the relationship of realized retirement consumption to that enjoyed at the end of worklife, can be indicated.

The data available for testing the model are far from satisfactory. Taking estimates of disposable personal incomes and propensities to consume by broad occupational groups, and assuming what by present standards seems an unrealistically high public retirement transfer, one finds that even the most parsimonious family falls somewhat short of target consumption and considerably short of consumption at the end of worklife. Families saving not all but half of their income increases in later worklife achieve even less: not quite three-fourths of the age-50 consumption and only 58 percent of the level they enjoyed at the time of retirement. Families which make no change in their marginal propensities to consume during their last 15 years of worklife attain less than half their age-50 consumption during retirement and only a little more than a third of the level achieved at the end of worklife.[6] In all cases, it was assumed that home equity, along with liquid assets, was prorated over the retire-

---

6. James H. Schulz has estimated that about three-fourths of the males and one-half of the unmarried females have projected P/E ratios (defined as the ratio of retirement pension income to preretirement average earnings) of less than 0.50. See his "Aged Retirement Income Adequacy: Simulation Projections of Pension-Earnings Ratios," Joint Economic Committee, *Old Age Income Assurance*, 90th Congress, 1st session, 1967, pp. 245–259.

ment period, although in reality such an option may not prevail.

It is clear that changes in any one of several values would serve to move ex post consumption closer to ex ante consumption: incomes could rise faster; worklife could be extended; the planning period could begin earlier. Conversely, a lowering of retirement age (or an increase in life expectancy, with retirement age remaining at 65), or a slower rate of income growth, or failure to hold consumption to the age-50 level would reduce retirement incomes. A lowering of retirement age could theoretically be offset by increased annual savings; yet increased savings by individual families seem quite unlikely.

In the solution of the low-income problem in old age, the role that can be played by private savings would appear to be a very limited one for families whose incomes during worklife fall below the median. The estimates derived in the foregoing examples illustrate the constraint imposed by income at the median level, demonstrating that even when the marginal propensity to save is quite high (one-half, for example, or when half the income increases received after age 50 are saved for retirement), savings adequate to maintain the targeted level of consumption are not forthcoming. But we know that for most families the marginal propensity to save is in fact much lower, and this inability to save reduces even further the significance of voluntary savings as a source of retirement income.

The failure to save for old age is understandable; incomes, although rising, are not increasing as fast as aspirations, particularly those of lower socioeconomic groups. Private pension growth could ease the problem by giving workers a growing portion of their earnings in retirement income claims, rather than current wages. If this form of forced saving were more widely used, with coverage extended to the lower-income worker, society could rely more heavily on industry to effect the necessary reapportionment of income between the working and nonworking years. However, present coverage is quite limited, and it is estimated that only 25 to 30 percent of the retirees will have private pension claims by 1975.[7]

Transfers between workers as a group and retirees as a group, which occur through the OASDHI tax-benefit arrangement, now provide the major source of retirement income. By paying a payroll tax during worklife, one guarantees his own right to a subsequent benefit, and thus in a sense he is forced to "save" for retirement. The benefit received, moreover, is somewhat related to past earnings and hence to the amount of tax paid during worklife. Since there is no auto-

7. See Joseph Krislov, "Employee-Benefit Plans, 1954–62," *Social Security Bulletin,* 27 (April, 1964), 16–20.

matic mechanism for adjusting benefit to changes in either prices or the growth in per capita income, there is a tendency for this portion of retirement income to lag behind living costs, and further still behind the real income of workers. If we are to rely on public benefits to bring retirees' incomes more nearly into line with either their own past earnings or the earnings of the now active workers, it would seem to be necessary to relate benefits to the growth in per capita income.[8]

8. For an analysis of the manner in which the West German social insurance system links pension levels to economic growth, see Gaston Rimlinger, "Social Insurance and Economic Growth: A Model of the German System," Joint Economic Committee, *Old Age Income Assurance,* Part II: *The Aged Population and Retirement Income Programs,* pp. 357–361.

APPENDIX: ESTIMATES OF RETIREMENT INCOME UNDER THREE SAVINGS VARIANTS

THE PARSIMONIOUS VARIANT

Calculations based on the BLS income data yield the estimates (exclusive of home ownership) for all occupational groups combined, under the *parsimonious variant* (see Table 11.1).

The average disposable personal income for families with heads aged 50 in 1970 is $6,774 (line 1). Average disposable personal income of families with heads aged 65 in 1975 is $9,117 (line 2). The total increase in disposable personal income during the last 15 years of worklife, under the 2 percent annual growth assumption, is $2,343 (line 3). This is an annual increase of $156 (line 4). Target consumption is DPI at age 50 times the average propensity to consume, or $6,774 times 0.91, or $6,164 (line 5).

On the assumption that OASDI benefits are $2,500 annually,[1] the gap between targeted consumption and benefits is $3,664 (line 6). This income gap must be met from the savings and interest thereon accumulated during the last 15 years of worklife. Assets required to provide an annual income of $3,664 for 15 years, thereby filling the gap between target consumption and income transfers, total $35,585

1. The assumption of retirement benefits is liberal; the 1967 average monthly benefit for an aged couple was $142. The 1967 increases in social security benefits bring this average up to $163.30. See *Hearings before the Committee on Ways and Means,* House of Representatives, 90th Congress, 1st session on H.R. 5710, March, 1967, Part I, pp. 101–102.

Table 11.1. Estimated retirement incomes for families with heads aged 45–54 in 1960–1961, excluding home equity (*parsimonious variant*)

	Total	Self-employed	Salaried professionals and officials	Clerical and sales	Wage earners		
					Skilled	Semi-skilled	Unskilled
1. Income at age 50	$ 6,774	$ 7,292	$10,408	$ 6,733	$ 6,955	$ 5,897	$ 4,272
2. Income at age 65	9,117	9,814	14,008	9,062	9,360	7,937	5,740
3. Total increase in income	2,343	2,522	3,600	2,329	2,405	2,040	1,478
4. Annual increase in income	156	168	240	155	160	136	99
5. Targeted consumption	6,164	6,636	7,077	6,127	6,329	5,661	4,272
6. Retirement income deficit	3,664	4,136	4,577	3,627	3,829	3,161	1,772
7. Retirement assets needed	35,585	40,169	44,453	35,226	37,188	30,700	17,210
8. Retirement assets available	25,258	27,044	38,771	25,078	25,922	21,917	15,895
9. Prorated available assets	2,600	2,784	3,992	2,582	2,669	2,256	1,636
10. Potential income	5,100	5,284	6,492	5,082	5,169	4,756	4,136
11. Potential incomes as a percentage of targeted consumption	82.7%	79.6%	91.7%	82.9%	81.6%	84.0%	96.8%
12. Potential incomes as a percentage of consumption at age 65	66.5%	64.0%	68.1%	66.7%	65.7%	71.3%	74.9%
13. Total asset deficit	$10,327	$13,125	$ 5,682	$10,148	$11,266	$ 8,783	$ 1,315
14. Annual asset deficit	1,063	1,351	585	1,045	1,160	904	132
15. Ex post consumption	5,101	5,285	6,492	5,082	5,169	4,757	4,140
16. Additional savings needed at 64	133	169	73	635	646	595	518
17. Total savings needed at 64	2,476	2,691	3,673	2,964	3,051	2,635	1,996
18. Implied income at 64	9,250	9,983	14,081	9,697	10,006	8,532	6,268
19. Implied annual income increase	165	179	245	198	203	176	133
20. Implied annual growth rate	2.09%	2.13%	2.16%	2.48%	2.45%	2.49%	2.61%

Source: Calculated from United States Department of Labor, Bureau of Labor Statistics, *Survey of Consumer Expenditures, 1960–61; Cross-classification of Family Characteristics: Total United States, Urban and Rural, 1960–1961.* table 15d, p. 33. Washington: Government Printing Office, 1966.

(line 7). Assets available at retirement (not counting home equity) total $25,258 (line 8). When these assets are prorated for the 15 years of retirement, they add $2,600 to annual income (line 9). Potential income during retirement is therefore the sum of transfers ($2,500) and annual income from assets ($2,600), or $5,100 (line 10). This potential income of $5,100 is 82.7 percent of the targeted consumption of $6,164 (line 11). It is 66.5 percent of the consumption level at age 65 (91.1 percent of $9,117, or $8,306) when retirement begins (line 12).

Deducting total assets available at age 65 (line 8), or $25,258, from those required to maintain targeted consumption during retirement (line 7), or $35,585, yields a total asset deficit at age 65 of $10,327 (line 13). Prorating this asset deficit over the retirement period results in an annual asset deficit of $1,063 (line 14). Actual consumption, then, must fall below targeted consumption to an amount equal to $6,164, minus $1,063, or $5,101, which is identical with potential income (line 15). If targeted consumption is to be attained, total savings at age 65 must rise by $133 (line 16), or to a total of $2,476 (line 17).[2] Only if income at age 65 is $9,250 can a savings of $2,476 be forthcoming (line 18). For income at end of worklife to be $9,250, the average annual increase in income must be $165 (line 19). An average annual increase in income of $165 requires the rate of growth of income to be 2.09 percent per year (line 20).

When the home value is prorated for 15 years, and the income added to the estimated potential income derived above, the following income increases occur (Table 11.2):

Potential income is $5,100 (line 1) as derived in Table 11.1. The prorated home value[3] adds $665 per year to potential income (line 2), which gives a total potential income of $5,765 per year (line 3). This potential income is 93.5 percent of targeted consumption, or consumption at age 50 (line 4); and 75.2 percent of consumption at the beginning of retirement period (line 5). The total asset deficit, as computed in Table 11.1, is reduced to $4,327, when we add the median value of home equity of $6,000[4] to the assets accumulated at age 65 ($25,258) from Table 11.1 (line 6). Prorating this deficit over

2. It will be recalled that his requisite ending-year income is computed on the assumption that income (and, hence, saving) increases linearly.

3. The prorated value of the home is a residual derived by subtracting the income of married couples, with prorated assets, excluding home equity (or $3,130) from the incomes of married couples, with prorated assets, including home equity ($3,795). See Epstein and Murray, *The Aged Population of the United States,* p. 71.

4. Ibid., table 4.21, p. 323.

Table 11.2. Estimated retirement incomes for families with heads aged 45–54 in 1960–1961, including home equity (*parsimonious variant*)

	Total	Self-employed	Salaried professionals and officials[1]	Clerical and sales	Wage earners		
					Skilled	Semi-skilled	Unskilled
1. Potential income	$5,100	$5,284	$6,492	$5,082	$5,169	$4,756	$4,136
2. Prorated home value [b]	665	665	665	665	665	665	665
3. Total potential income	5,765	5,949	7,157	5,747	5,834	5,421	4,801
4. Total potential incomes as a percentage of targeted consumption	93.5%	89.6%	101.1%	93.7%	92.1%	95.7%	112.3%
5. Total potential incomes as a percentage of consumption at age 65	75.2%	72.1%	75.1%	75.4%	74.2%	81.3%	86.9%
6. Total asset deficit	$4,327	$7,125	–$ 318	$4,148	$5,266	$2,783	–$4,685
7. Annual asset deficit	445	734	— 33	427	542	286	— 482
8. Ex-post consumption	5,719	5,902	7,110	5,770	5,787	5,375	4,754
9. Additional savings needed at age 64	54	89	— 40	5	7	3	— 6
10. Total savings needed at age 64	2,397	2,432	2,339	2,348	2,350	2,346	2,289
11. Implied income at age 64	9,171	9,206	9,113	9,122	9,124	9,126	9,063
12. Implied annual income increase	158	162	156	156	156	156	153
13. Implied annual growth rate	2.088%	2.21%	1.85%	2.19%	2.17%	2.20%	1.84%

[a] Since we have assumed an extremely low value of APC (0.68) for salaried professionals and officials, we get aberrant results when home equity is included. Specifically, we find that potential income exceeds the low targeted consumption; consequently, the assets deficit becomes a surplus, and targeted consumption can be increased. Alternatively, savings at age 64 could be decreased, or the average annual rate of growth of income could be reduced.

[b] The addition of *median* value of home equity serves to raise total assets of unskilled workers to unrealistically high levels. This results in the following distorted estimates: total potential income exceeds targeted consumption; there is now an asset surplus, making possible either an increase in ex post consumption or a decrease in savings at age 64. Inasmuch as the value of a home owned by the lower-income earner probably reflects low lifetime earnings, more reliable estimates would be yielded by data on home value by income level of owner.

Source: Calculated from Lenore A. Epstein and Janet H. Murray, *The Aged Population of the United States*, Department of Health, Education, and Welfare, Social Security Administration Report 19, 1967.

the remaining expected years of life yields an annual asset deficit of $445 (line 7). Consequently, ex post consumption must fall to $6,164 — $445, or $5,719 (line 8).

In order that targeted consumption obtain, $54 additional savings must be acquired in the last year of working life (line 9), implying total savings at age 65 of $2,397 (line 10). Consequently, income in the last working year must be $9,171 (line 11), which is an average annual increase in income of $158 (line 12). The average annual income increase will be forthcoming only if the rate of growth of income is 2.088 percent (line 13).

When the *parsimonious* family attempts to smooth consumption between the ages of 50 and 65, saving all income increments for consumption during retirement, it can actually save but $25,258. When prorated over the remaining lifespan, this amount will add $2,600 to annual income, resulting in a total consumption of $5,100. Retirement consumption is 83 percent of age-50 consumption (of $6,184) and only 66 percent of the potential consumption at age 65 ($8,306, or 91 percent of the income, $9,117).

When the prorated home value is added to income, retirement consumption would reach about 93 percent of age-50 and 75 percent of age-64 consumption.

THE PRACTICAL VARIANT

From the *practical variant,* in which the family consumes half the increments in income accruing after age 50, we derive the following estimates (Table 11.3):

Assets accumulated at age 65 will total $13,629 in value (line 1): this asset accumulation adds $1,300 to annual income (line 2) during retirement. Potential income is therefore $2,500 plus $1,300, or $3,800 per year (line 3), which is 61.6 percent of consumption at age 50, or targeted consumption (line 4), and 49.6 percent of consumption at age 65 (line 5). Total asset deficit at age 65 is $22,956 (line 6), which is an annual asset deficit during retirement of $2,364. Realized consumption during retirement can be only $3,800 (line 8). If targeted consumption is to obtain, additional savings at age 65 must amount to $2,869 (line 9), and total savings must be $5,212 (line 10). This implies an income in the last year of working life of $11,986 (line 11) and an average annual income increase of $347 (line 12); these savings necessitate an annual growth in income of 3.89 percent (line 13).

Table 11.3. Estimated retirement incomes for families with heads aged 45–54 in 1960–1961, excluding home equity (*practical variant*)

	Total	Self-employed	Salaried professionals and officials	Clerical and sales	Wage earners		
					Skilled	Semiskilled	Unskilled
1. Retirement assets available	$12,629	$13,522	$19,385	$12,539	$12,961	$10,959	$7,948
2. Annual asset decumulation	1,300	1,392	1,996	1,291	1,334	1,128	818
3. Potential income	3,800	3,892	4,496	3,791	3,834	3,628	3,318
4. Potential income as a percentage of targeted consumption	61.6%	59.6%	63.5%	61.9%	60.6%	64.1%	77.7%
5. Potential income as a percentage of consumption at age 65	49.6%	47.2%	47.2%	49.8%	48.7%	54.4%	60.1%
6. Total asset deficit	$22,956	$26,647	$25,068	$22,687	$24,227	$19,741	$9,262
7. Annual asset deficit	2,364	2,744	2,581	2,336	2,494	2,033	953
8. Ex post consumption	3,800	3,892	4,496	3,791	3,835	3,628	3,319
9. Additional savings needed at age 65	2,869	3,331	3,133	2,836	3,028	2,468	1,158
10. Total savings needed at age 65	5,212	5,853	6,739	5,165	5,433	4,508	2,636
11. Implied income at age 65	11,986	13,145	17,147	11,898	12,388	10,405	6,908
12. Implied annual increase in income	347	390	449	344	362	301	176
13. Implied annual growth rate	3.89%	4.02%	3.38%	3.89%	3.98%	3.89%	3.25%

Source: Calculated from table 11.1.

Adding the prorated home value (Table 11.4), we find that the potential income of $3,800 (line 1) estimated above, plus the $665 annual income from the home (line 2), yields a potential income of $4,465 (line 3); this is 72.4 percent of age-50 consumption (line 4), and 58.3 percent of consumption at the end of worklife (line 5). The addition of median value of home equity to assets accumulated at age 65 reduces the total asset deficit to $16,956 (line 6), which is an annual asset deficit during retirement of $1,746 (line 7). Ex post consumption must then total to $4,418 during the remaining lifespan (line 8). Alternatively, if targeted consumption is to be realized, savings at age 65 must be increased by $2,219 (line 9), to total savings in the last year of working life of $4,462 (line 10), which implies that income at age 65 is $11,236 (line 11). The implied average annual increase in income of $297 (line 12) will be forthcoming only if the average annual rate of growth in income is 3.43 percent (line 13).

THE PROFLIGATE VARIANT

Similarly, for the *profligate variant,* in which the family continues to increase its consumption in accordance with its increase in disposable income after age 50, we derive the following results (Table 11.5):

Disposable personal income at age 65 is $9,117 (line 1, as calculated in Table 11.1). Consumption at age 65 is therefore $7,658, or $9,117 multiplied by the applicable value of B, or 0.875, for column 1 (line 2). Assets, accumulated between ages 50 and 65 at an annual rate of interest of 6 percent, will be lower than obtained with lower values of B: specifically, assets accumulated at age 65 (excluding home) in the *parsimonious variant,* multiplied by $1 - B$, or $25,258 multiplied by $1 - 0.875$. This gives the $3,410 of line 3.

Prorating accumulated assets over the retirement period adds $351 to annual income during this period (line 4). Potential income is therefore $2,500 plus $351, or $2,851 per year (line 5), which is 46.2 percent of consumption at age 50—that is, 46.2 percent of targeted consumption (line 6) and 37.2 percent of consumption at the end of worklife (line 7). The total asset deficit is $32,175 (line 8), which is an annual asset deficit of $3,312 (line 9). Therefore, realized consumption during retirement must fall to $2,852 (line 10). For targeted consumption to obtain during retirement, savings at age 64 must rise by $4,022 (line 11), and total savings in the last year of

Table 11.4. Estimated retirement incomes for families with heads aged 45–54 in 1960–1961, including home equity (*practical variant*)

	Total	Self-employed	Salaried professionals and officials	Clerical and sales	Wage earners		
					Skilled	Semiskilled	Unskilled
1. Potential income	$ 3,800	$ 3,892	$ 4,496	$ 3,791	$ 3,834	$ 3,628	$3,318
2. Prorated home value	665	665	665	665	665	665	665
3. Potential income	4,465	4,557	5,161	4,456	4,499	4,293	3,983
4. Potential incomes as a percentage of targeted consumption	72.4%	68.6%	72.9%	72.7%	70.2%	75.8%	93.2%
5. Potential incomes as a percentage of consumption at age 65	58.3%	55.2%	54.1%	58.5%	57.2%	64.3%	72.1%
6. Total asset deficit	$16,956	$20,647	$19,068	$16,687	$18,224	$13,743	$3,262
7. Annual asset deficit	1,746	2,126	1,963	1,718	1,876	1,415	3,359
8. Ex post consumption	4,418	4,510	5,114	4,409	4,453	4,246	913
9. Additional savings needed at age 64	2,119	2,580	2,383	2,086	2,278	1,718	408
10. Total savings needed at age 64	4,462	5,102	5,983	4,415	4,683	3,758	1,886
11. Implied income at age 64	11,236	12,394	16,391	11,148	11,638	9,655	6,158
12. Implied annual income increase	297	340	399	294	312	251	126
13. Implied annual growth rate	3.43%	3.61%	3.09%	3.46%	3.50%	3.36%	2.49%

Source: Calculated from table 11.2.

Table 11.5. Estimated retirement incomes for families with heads aged 45–54 in 1960–1961, excluding home equity (*profligate variant*)

	Total	Self-employed	Salaried professionals and officials	Clerical and sales	Wage earners		
					Skilled	Semiskilled	Unskilled
1. Income at 65	$ 9,117	$ 9,814	$14,008	$ 9,062	$ 9,360	$ 7,937	$ 5,750
2. Consumption at 65	7,658	8,244	9,525	7,612	7,862	6,667	5,520
3. Retirement assets available	3,410	3,651	12,406	3,386	3,499	2,192	318
4. Annual asset decumulation	351	375	1,277	348	360	226	33
5. Potential income	2,851	2,875	3,777	2,848	2,860	2,726	2,533
6. Potential income as a percentage of targeted consumption	46.2%	43.3%	53.3%	46.4%	45.1%	48.1%	59.2%
7. Potential income as a percentage of consumption at 65	37.2%	34.8%	39.6%	37.4%	36.3%	40.8%	45.8%
8. Total asset deficit	$32,175	$36,518	$32,047	$31,840	$33,689	$28,508	$16,892
9. Annual asset deficit	3,312	3,760	3,300	3,278	3,469	2,935	1,739
10. Ex post consumption	2,282	2,876	3,777	2,849	2,860	2,726	2,533
11. Additional savings needed at 65	4,022	4,565	4,006	3,980	4,211	3,563	2,112
12. Total savings needed at 65	6,365	7,087	7,612	6,309	6,616	5,603	3,590
13. Implied income at 65	13,139	14,379	18,020	13,042	13,571	11,500	7,862
14. Implied annual increase in income	424	472	507	421	441	374	239
15. Implied annual growth rate	4.54%	4.64%	3.75%	4.53%	4.59%	4.58%	4.17%

Source: Calculated from table 11.1.

Table 11.6. Estimated retirement incomes for families with heads aged 45–54 in 1960–1961, including home equity (*profligate variant*)

	Total	Self-employed	Salaried professionals and officials	Clerical and sales	Wage earners		
					Skilled	Semiskilled	Unskilled
1. Potential income	$ 2,851	$ 2,875	$ 3,777	$ 2,848	$ 2,860	$ 2,726	$ 2,533
2. Prorated home value	665	665	665	665	665	665	665
3. Total potential income	3,516	3,540	4,442	3,513	3,525	3,391	3,198
4. Total potential incomes as a percentage of targeted consumption	57.0%	53.3%	62.8%	57.3%	55.7%	59.9%	74.8%
5. Total potential incomes as a percentage of consumption at age 65	45.9%	42.9%	46.6%	46.1%	44.8%	50.9%	57.9%
6. Total asset deficit	$26,175	$30,518	$26,047	$25,840	$27,689	$22,508	$10,892
7. Annual asset deficit	2,695	3,142	2,682	2,660	2,851	2,317	1,121
8. Ex post consumption	3,469	3,494	4,395	3,467	3,478	3,344	3,151
9. Additional savings needed at age 64	3,272	3,815	3,256	3,230	3,461	2,813	1,362
10. Total savings needed at age 64	5,615	6,337	6,856	5,559	5,866	4,853	2,840
11. Implied income at age 64	12,389	13,629	17,264	12,292	12,821	10,750	7,112
12. Implied annual income increase	374	422	457	371	391	324	189
13. Implied annual growth rate	4.09%	4.25%	3.42%	4.08%	4.18%	4.09%	3.45%

Source: Calculated from table 11.2.

Table 11.7. Summary of retirement income estimates for 1975, United States totals

	Y_R / C_T	Retirement asset deficit		Income at age 64	Savings at age 64		Implied income at age 64	Implied annual growth rate
		Total	Annual		Actual	Required		
Parsimonious consumption variant (APS = 1.0)								
Excluding home equity	82.7%	$10,327	$1,063	$9,117	$2,343	$2,476	$ 9,250	2.099%
Including home equity	93.5%	4,327	445	9,117	2,343	2,397	9,171	2.088%
Practical consumption variant (APS = 0.50)								
Excluding home equity	61.6%	22,956	2,364	9,117	2,343	5,212	11,986	3.89%
Including home equity	72.4%	16,956	1,746	9,117	2,343	4,462	11,236	3.43%
Profligate consumption variant (APS = 0.125)								
Excluding home equity	46.2%	32,175	3,312	9,117	2,343	6,365	13,139	4.54%
Including home equity	45.9%	26,175	2,695	9,117	2,343	5,615	12,389	4.09%

Source: Tables 11.1–11.6.

worklife must be $6,365 (line 12). Such savings will be forthcoming only if income in the last working year is $13,139 (line 13). This necessitates an average annual increase in income of $424 (line 14), which implies an annual average rate of growth in income of 4.54 percent (line 15).

If we prorate the value of the home for 15 years, adding this income to that derived above, we see the following increases in estimated potential income (Table 11.6):

Potential income is $2,851, as derived in Table 11.5 (line 1). The prorated home value is $665, as in Table 11.2 (line 2), yielding a total potential income of $3,516 per year (line 3), which is 57 percent of targeted consumption, or consumption at age 50 (line 4), and 45.9 percent of consumption at the end of the worklife (line 5). The total asset deficit is reduced by the value of home equity and is then $26,175 (line 6), which is an annual asset deficit of $2,695 (line 7). This necessitates a reduction in ex post consumption of $3,469 during each year of retirement (line 8). On the other hand, if targeted consumption is to be maintained, savings at age 65 must be $3,272 (line 9), so that total savings at age 65 are $5,615 (line 10). This implies an income in the last year of working life of $12,389 (line 11) and an annual average income increase of $374 (line 12). These savings require an average annual rate of growth of income of 4.09 percent (line 13).

Table 11.7 summarizes the data for the three income variants as presented in detail in the preceding tables.

IV. WORK AND INCOME ALLOCATION IN THE UNITED STATES: POLICY CONSIDERATIONS

12. ECONOMIC GROWTH AND INCOME THROUGH THE LIFE CYCLE

The constraints on saving for the retirement period become evident on examination of the pattern of income and expenditures through the successive stages of the family cycle. Even for families receiving more than the median income, expenditures are likely to be higher than income during the decade after family formation, in part because of the purchase of consumer durables and initial payments on a home. These purchases are only partly current expense; they continue to serve the family during subsequent years, in the case of the home, even during retirement. But except for home investment and perhaps some savings in the form of life insurance, families do not often acquire savings during this early stage.

Increases in earnings that accrue to the family head during his late thirties and forties are again matched by expenditures, this time for children's education and, not infrequently, partial support of aged parents. Until children are self-supporting, low-income families find it impossible and moderate-income families quite difficult to make any financial preparations for retirement. For this reason, the model developed in the two preceding chapters assumed that systematic savings for old age began at age 50, these privately held funds being in addition to home equity and public retirement benefit claims acquired during working years.

As the earlier illustrations of average-income families show, a significant drop in consumption is likely to be necessary at the time of retirement, even with stringent savings during the last 15 years of worklife. Exceptions occur for those families having substantial private pension claims. Workers who have low earnings, or who suffer disability, unemployment, or other adversity during the last decade of worklife, will face retirement with little or no savings, and with less than the maximum OASDHI benefit assumed in these examples.

The longer the savings period, the greater a family's chances of acquiring savings adequate for retirement. But regardless of the length of the savings period, the saver's economic position relative to that of persons in the labor force is likely to be inferior, since his savings were some proportion of earlier, lower earnings; the worker, meanwhile, continues to enjoy the gains from economic growth. A summary statement of the impact of growth on the retiree's economic status follows.

ECONOMIC GROWTH AND RETIREMENT INCOMES: A HYPOTHETICAL CASE

It is widely recognized (and applauded) that technological advance and capital accumulation produce rising incomes per capita and per employee over time. In the United States disposable real income per capita rose at an average rate of 1.9 percent per year during the 1946–1966 period. Not so widely recognized is the fact that under most systems of providing income for the aged, there will be a tendency for incomes of retired persons to lag well behind those of employed persons.

John O. Blackburn has illustrated the lag with a simple model.[1] Suppose that all income earners save systematically for their own retirements. More specifically, assume that from any given year's income the recipient sets aside that fraction necessary to provide a retirement level of consumption equal to the level *of that year*. Note that the model does not specify the amount of saving necessary for retirement consumption at one-third, one-half, or two-thirds of working consumption; rather, it aims at matching working consumption dollar for dollar.

Suppose further that each worker's income is rising at rate m per year. He will save a constant fraction of each year's income, the objective being to maintain that year's consumption level during retirement, and the assumption being that the current year's income will prevail throughout worklife. Upon retirement, he takes his savings (the cumulated sum plus interest on an annual contribution

---

1. See Kreps and Blackburn, "The Impact of Economic Growth on Retirement Incomes," pp. 58–64.

that has risen at rate *m* per year throughout worklife, since he has saved each year a constant share of income rising at rate *m* per year) and buys an annuity providing whatever annual income can be purchased for the remainder of his life.

But whereas he then has a fixed payment per year for as long as he lives, persons in the labor force continue to enjoy rising incomes at rate *m* per year. In such a model the retiree will always be consuming less than the worker (even when the worker saves at a rate sufficient, he thinks, to maintain his current level of consumption), since the retiree's savings were accumulated during an earlier period when earnings were lower than those of the present generation of workers.

Table 12.1. Consumption expenditures of new retirees as a proportion of consumption expenditures of workers, at various rates, on income growth

Rate of income growth (*m*)	Retirees' consumption (*percentage of workers' consumption*)
.00	100
.01	77
.02	60
.03	48
.04	35

The relation between the level of consumption of retirees and that of workers depends, *ceteris paribus,* on the rate of income advance *m*. For some numerical examples, let us suppose that the average age of entry to the labor force is 20, retirement occurs at age 60, and death at age 80. On the average, therefore, people work 40 years and have 20 years of retirement. Further assume the relevant rate of interest to be 5 percent. Consumption at the beginning of the retirement period, as a proportion of the average consumption of workers, would then be 100 percent only if *m* were zero (Table 12.1). If per capita income grows at 2 percent, however, the retirement consumption level is only 60 percent of that enjoyed by workers.

But even this proportion of consumption is not maintained for retirees during their retirement period. Incomes of workers continue to grow, and retirement incomes become smaller fractions during the two decades of retirement. If the annual rate of income growth is 2 percent, retirement consumption halfway through the period has fallen to 45 percent of the workers' consumption level, and by the

Table 12.2 Retirees' consumption after 5, 10, 15, and 20 years of retirement, as a proportion of workers' consumption (*income growth rates of .02
and .03*)

Years in retirement	Retirees' consumption (*percentage of workers' consumption*)	
	.02 rate of growth	.03 rate of growth
0	60	48
5	52	41
10	45	36
15	39	31
20	33	27

end of life the proportion is only one-third (Table 12.2). If incomes
are rising at a rate of 3 percent annually, the relative deterioration of
retirement consumption occurs even faster. From a 48 percent level at
the beginning of retirement, consumption falls to 36 percent after ten
years and eventually to 27 percent of the workers' level.

Under these assumptions, then, an annual rate of saving aimed at
providing retirement consumption equal to 100 percent of current
consumption during worklife would in fact provide only a fraction
—perhaps one-half to two-thirds—of consumption during worklife,
and this proportion at the beginning of the retirement period. During the course of the retirement years, the retiree's level of consumption falls further still, perhaps to as little as one-fourth of that enjoyed
by persons still at work. Figure 12.1 illustrates the relative deterioration in the aged's consumption level during a 20-year retirement
period, assuming a 2 percent annual growth rate.

ECONOMIC GROWTH AND RETIREMENT INCOMES: PAST AND FUTURE

Earnings constitute a significant source of income for the aged—
nearly a third of the total—despite the low labor force participation
rate of older men. But since so few persons in their seventies or
eighties continue working, the bulk of the aged's earnings accrue to
the younger family heads in the group, those aged 65 through 69.
Thus, although social security and other public benefits make up
only about 40 percent of the aged's aggregate income, such pensions
are likely to be the major (often the only) source of income for the
oldest group, who are much more frequently in financial need.

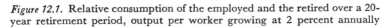

Figure 12.1. Relative consumption of the employed and the retired over a 20-year retirement period, output per worker growing at 2 percent annually

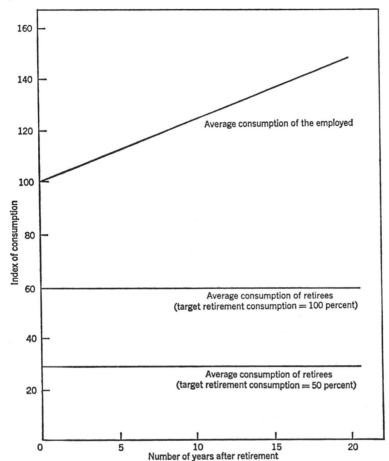

During the first half of the 1960s, the income position of the elderly appears to have worsened somewhat relative to that of young families, which is consistent with the Blackburn model. While the money incomes of all age groups have been rising since 1960, those of older families have not increased as much as the incomes of the under-65 age group. The median income for families with heads under 65 increased by $2,000, or 34 percent, from 1960 through 1966, but families with heads over 65 have seen an increase of only $750, or 26 percent. Aged unrelated individuals gained relative to younger single persons in 1961–1962, but lost ground thereafter; since 1962, the median income of elderly individuals has risen 16 percent, which is about half the percentage increase for younger persons.

The question thus arises as to the future growth in retirement incomes, and the relationship of that growth to the probable increase in the incomes of the active population. Earlier, Schulz [2] concluded from a simulation projection that in 1980 about half the couples and more than four-fifths of the unmarried retirees will receive $3,000 or less in annual pension income, both public and private. Three-fourths of the couples will be receiving pension incomes of $4,000 or less, with only about one-eighth having pensions of more than $5,000. When the 1980 estimates are corrected for price change (assuming that the 1955–1965 price rise of 1.6 percent yearly continues till 1980), 81 percent of the retired couples are expected to have a real pension income plus asset income of $4,000 or less; the comparable proportion for 1962 was 84 percent. Continuation of past rates of growth in pension benefits, or even some slight acceleration in rate,[3] will thus probably do little more than offset price rises.

ALLOCATING THE GAINS FROM ECONOMIC GROWTH

Not only is the accumulation of private savings in sufficient amounts to keep retirement incomes in step with earnings extremely difficult; there is in the present scheme of income allocation, which offers rewards primarily on the basis of productivity, the implicit assumption that the gains from economic growth are due altogether to the efforts of persons who are currently at work. In reality, increases in the productivity of the worker may have very little to do with his own actions and initiative; they result, rather, from capital accumulation and advances in technology. The growth component of increases in income is largely fortuitous from the standpoint of the individual worker.

Income gains from intraoccupational promotions and from advances into higher occupational categories, which are due to knowledge and job experience, are the rewards for individual effort. Further increments accrue to those persons who are willing to undergo

2. James H. Schulz, "The Future Economic Circumstances of the Aged: A Simulation Projection," *Yale Economic Essays*, 7 (Spring, 1967), 145–217.

3. In the study cited, social security benefits were assumed to increase by 4 percent annually between 1962 and 1980. Ibid., p. 211.

extended education and training. The income differentials attributable to education, skill, and experience, however, can be maintained without also imputing to the current generation of workers that portion of output that derives from scientific and technological progress.

Offsets to their relative decline in income will be available only insofar as older persons are able to continue working, at least on a part-time basis, or retirement benefits (public and private) grow in some rough accord with the overall growth of the economy. Arrangements for tying social security benefits to the cost of living, although an important safeguard in periods of inflation, will not meet the need to keep retirement benefits in line with earnings. A central question comes to be, then: To what extent (and through what mechanisms) are retired persons to share in the growth in the national product?

In earlier studies, Joseph J. Spengler analyzed the alternative methods of distributing the gains from technical progress.[4] In the first instance, he points out, rising real incomes can accrue to all persons in the society through a gradual reduction in prices. Everyone who is a consumer then shares the benefits of growth; money wages remain essentially unchanged, while the purchasing power of these wages rises as the prices of goods decline. But this method of diffusing the growing output has had little support in recent decades, primarily because falling prices are frequently associated with slower growth and higher levels of unemployment than policy-makers have thought necessary.

If costs and prices do not decline as output increases, money incomes may rise in accordance with the productivity increase. Real incomes from wages, profits, and rent thus reflect ,the growth, with investors sharing in the increase insofar as they hold equities. But whereas persons with fixed-income claims share in the gains from growth in the case of falling prices, they do not share in the rise in money incomes. Instead, their real incomes steadily fall behind. Thus, with the help of monetary and fiscal measures, the growth in output accrues to those currently active in producing it, either with their labor or their capital investments.

Spengler argues that

4. See "Wage-Price Movements and Old-Age Security," in I. L. Webber, *Aging: A Current Appraisal* (Gainesville, Fla.: University of Florida Institute of Gerontology, 1956) , esp. pp. 110–116; also Juanita M. Kreps and Joseph J. Spengler, "Equity and Social Credit for the Retired," in Kreps, *Employment, Income, and Retirement Problems of the Aged* (Durham, N.C.: Duke University Press, 1963) , pp. 198–229.

some but by no means all of technical progress is imputable to
those who presently garner its fruits. Technical progress is largely
the result of the application of accumulating scientific knowledge, an essentially communal product, together with improvement in the human factor and residual forces which may be
assembled under the head of "increasing return." [5]

As an equitable solution he suggests that retirees be provided some
share in the growth in output through the establishment of a social
credit scheme, in accordance with which their retirement benefits rise
by, say, 1 percent per year.

A social credit arrangement of this sort has never been seriously
considered in the United States, although a similar rationale is inherent in the West German social insurance system. In a recent
analysis of that scheme, Gaston Rimlinger points out that pensions
are expected to maintain for the retiree the relative standard of living he enjoyed during worklife. Accordingly, since the scheme was
reorganized in 1957, pensions have been adjusted annually to the
rate of economic growth, maintaining "both the relative position of
the individual and of all pensioners." [6] Since pensions rise with increases in national income, contributions also rise; the taxable base
is two and a half times the average earnings of covered workers. As
Rimlinger notes, the German system significantly reallocates income
from workers to pensioners.

LEVELS OF LIVING: RELATIVE OR ABSOLUTE?

The income issues arising in a period of rapid economic growth
are illustrated by our inability to agree on an "adequate" (or even
a "poverty") level of living. The definition of income adequacy is
elusive in at least one important respect: On what basis is adequacy
to be judged? Is there a market basket of goods that draws the dividing line between poverty and minimum well-being? If so, it can be
priced in various geographical locations, for families of different
sizes and age compositions. The dollar cost of maintaining a family
with a particular set of characteristics would then change to reflect
price change, but presumably not for other reasons. An adequate
standard is one which includes certain essentials of food, clothing,

5. Ibid., p. 224.
6. "Social Insurance and Economic Growth: A Model of the German System,"
in Joint Economic Committee, *Old Age Income Assurance*, Part II, pp. 357–361.

shelter, etc., and the required quantities of these commodities remain fixed.

Or is income adequacy properly defined in relation to the median income of a population? If median family income in 1968 is $8,000, are four-person families with less than half the median living in poverty? [7] With less than 40 percent of the median? Whatever the proportion specified, the actual dollar income will of course rise from year to year as the median grows. Since family income in this country has increased steadily throughout the past two decades, the poverty line by this definition has also been rising. To "graduate" out of poverty in 1968 would thus require a much higher money income and in fact a higher real income than in 1948; even when corrected for price changes, the 1968 poverty level would be higher than in any preceding year.

These two concepts of poverty are of particular significance in discussions of the economic position of the aged, and the effect of growth on that position. In brief, the real income of families, including most of those headed by elderly persons, is raised by technological advance and the growth it generates. But since most of the fruits of such growth accrue to persons still in the labor force, retirees' incomes (which are lower than earnings at the beginning of the retirement span) gradually deteriorate relative to those of the active population. If the retirement span is long and the rate of economic growth high, the ratio of the aged's retirement benefits to average earnings will be altered drastically during retirement, as the earlier model indicates.

This curious conclusion can thus be drawn: the faster the pace of technology and the higher the rate of economic growth, the greater is the disparity between earnings and retirement benefits, under present income-allocation arrangements. Hence, in a relative sense economic deprivation of the nonworking aged is generated in the process of technological advance and growth. Returning to the concept of deprivation on an absolute standard, however, the record is one of gradually rising levels of living for all age groups, including the aged. Figures cited earlier indicate that the median income for families with heads aged 65 or over increased somewhat during the 1960–1966 period; so, too, did the median for aged unrelated individuals. In both cases, the percentage increases were smaller for the older groups than for the young.

The income increases accruing to the young and the old during

7. For a discussion of relative versus absolute standards of poverty, and other conceptual issues involved in the analysis of economic deprivation, see *The Concept of Poverty* (Washington: United States Chamber of Commerce, 1965).

the early 1960s illustrate both the absolute and the relative effects of differential rates of income growth. In money income, the aged family's median rose by one-fourth; corrected for the Consumer Price Index increase, the real median increased by 11 percent. Yet because of the faster increase in the median income of younger families (34 percent), the rise in their real median was greater (20 percent), thereby widening the income gap between young and old.[8]

To illustrate further the impact of economic growth on the absolute level of the aged's income, one may rely on the poverty definitions developed by Mollie Orshansky of the Social Security Administration. Since the money income necessary to raise an aged couple above the poverty line was derived by summing the costs of a minimum basket of goods and services, a rise in real incomes of aged units enables some of these families to move out of poverty. One measure of the contribution of technology growth to reducing economic deprivation might be, in fact, the numbers of families each year that are able to move from poverty to a modest level of living.

Analysis would reveal the extent to which the elderly have been able to move out of Orshansky's two lowest-income groups (the poor and the near-poor) during the past two decades. Through time, there is a tendency for the nonworking poor to dominate the poverty group, if poverty is measured on an absolute basis. Eugene Smolensky has noted that "in a well-functioning and growing economy the proportion of the population living in poverty ought to fall, and those remaining in poverty ought, increasingly, to be characterized by somehow being outside the market process." [9] Certain groups (the aged and women household heads) are excluded from the normal economic process, he continues, because society does not want to draw them into the labor force. There are then two means of keeping them out: the mores of the state can exclude them involuntarily, or transfer payments can be made sufficiently attractive to remove an incentive to work. He concludes: "It is not clear that the former method, the one in primary use today, is more consistent with the free enterprise ethic than is the latter." [10]

8. Herman B. Brotman, "Incomes of Families and Unrelated Individuals, 1966," Administration on Aging, Department of Health, Education, and Welfare, 1967.

9. Eugene Smolensky, "The Past and Present Poor," in United States Chamber of Commerce, *The Concept of Poverty*, p. 45.

10. Ibid., p. 61.

13. FINANCING RETIREMENT INCOME

The dilemma of the aged person on a fixed income living alongside the wage earner whose pay reflects his rising productivity is one that results from both the drop in income attending retirement from work and the relative deterioration in income position during the retirement period. As Ida Merriam has pointed out, the latter problem has come to the forefront during the nation's period of sustained economic growth.

> For the income-maintenance programs . . . the difficult question posed by technological change and rising national income is not that of determining the benefit amounts of different individuals at the time they retire, but rather that of reaching a consensus as to what happens to their benefits over the subsequent 10, 15, or 20 years.[1]

If the incomes of retired persons are to be maintained at levels closer to those of economically active persons, whose earnings are always rising, how are such income supplements to be provided? There are few alternatives: one, private savings; two, private pension arrangements; and three, transfers via some taxation-benefit scheme. If retirement income is to be provided by public transfers, a major question remains: How is the transfer to be financed—by payroll taxes or from general revenues?

1. Ida C. Merriam, "Implications of Technological Change for Income," in Kreps, *Technology, Manpower, and Retirement Policy*, p. 171.

PRIVATE AND PUBLIC FINANCING

Most people agree that they should save substantial proportions of their incomes for retirement; most people fail to do so. The private method thus has the advantage of allowing a family to do its own lifetime budgeting and saving for old age; it has also the disadvantage of allowing it to do neither. Indeed, the widespread reliance on public and private pensions rests on the premise that many people make no voluntary systematic provisions for retirement income. Since people do not save enough to insure retirement incomes comparable to their current earnings, it is unrealistic to expect them to acquire savings adequate to match the even higher incomes of the future.

Private pension arrangements face much the same difficulty, since they also require more saving now for more consumption during retirement. In order to provide future benefits commensurate with future incomes and, further, provide benefits which would rise through the retirement period, private pension schemes would have to exact much heavier contributions from employers and employees than they now require. Unless these larger contributions are made, employers will find it difficult unilaterally to raise pension benefits above the levels financed by past contributions.

To the extent that financial support for retirement is not provided through the private sector, it must of course come from public income-maintenance schemes; controversy continues over the proper division of responsibility between the two sources. Yet dichotomizing man's individual productivity and that of society as alternative sources of support is misleading, since it suggests that the worker can evade responsibility for his retirement income and leave the matter to the government. Such a shift is not possible. The worker pays a tax throughout worklife, as does his employer (this portion of the tax being borne ultimately by the consumer in the form of a higher price or the worker in reduced money wage), and these revenues support persons then in retirement. When the worker retires, the generation at work is paying the tax, true, and the retiree receives benefits. But while the timing may make it appear that he is being supported by society—strictly speaking, all persons not at work or owning capital are being supported by society, since at the moment they are not contributing to output—this interpretation is not valid when considered within the context of man's lifetime.

The issue of public versus private financing of retirement is confused by questions of *who* provides the support and *when* he provides it. Increasingly, both young adults and aged persons acquire claims against the national product of any given year without contributing to that year's output via current membership in the labor force. In a broad sense, the young and old families may be considered the children and parents of the middle age group, who are the active participants in the production process and who, on a current basis, are the producers of the national output. Since current consumption must come from current output, it can be argued that parents in the middle age group are supporting both their adult offspring (and the families of these offspring) and their aged parents.

Intergenerational support thus conceived, however, is quite different from the traditional pattern in which the children and grandparents in each family were supported by the parents *of that family*. Support of one generation by another is increasingly provided, not within families, but between one whole generation and another. Thus the employed person in the middle age group contributes to the support of young adults via tax payments for financing education, and to the support of retired persons via the OASDI tax, whether or not he has children or retired parents.[2]

The middle-aged family head still has the option of saving for his own future retirement, in addition to the taxes he pays to support the young and the old generations. Whether he has the income to save is another question: Why has this option not been exercised more rigorously in the past? Has it been due to an inability to predict the future, or to the low levels of income, or to the fact that the wage earner's aspirations have outpaced his real income? These and other explanations abound. But little research has been devoted to the question why the present generation of retirees accumulated so little in savings. Even more important, study of the savings behavior of today's worker, which might reveal the extent to which future retirees will be able to rely on privately acquired income claims, is equally sparse.

FINANCING PUBLIC BENEFITS

Since the pattern of intergenerational support that is emerging is one wherein the generation rather than the individual family is the focal unit, the financial arrangements for the necessary transfers of in-

2. See the author's discussion in "The Economics of Intergenerational Relationships," pp. 267–288.

come are increasingly important. In particular, there is the question whether payroll taxes on employers and employees should continue to provide the funds for benefits, or whether benefits should be financed in part, at least, from general revenues.

The primary argument against the payroll tax is based on its regressivity, which places a burden on the low-income worker.[3] Since the tax at present applies to only the first $7,800 of earnings, the counterproposal of an increase in the taxable base (as opposed to further increase in the tax rate) is frequently made. Moreover, since the benefit is weighted in favor of the worker who has had low earnings, the regressive effect of the tax is somewhat mitigated. Arguing for the payroll tax is the advantage of having each worker feel that he is paying for his retirement benefit, which then comes to him as a right.

Revenues from the present payroll tax are insufficient to provide benefit increases of the magnitude necessary to improve significantly the aged's economic position. If benefits are to be raised, it is necessary either to increase taxes (by raising the rate or the taxable base) or to draw from general revenues. Yet further increases in the tax liability of the low-income worker are very hard to justify. If his income is at or below the poverty level, he now pays a tax on his earnings, although he is exempt from income tax payments precisely because we reason that his income is too low. When his employer's contribution is also considered—as a reduction in his wages or an increase in the prices he pays—the combined tax will ultimately reduce his income by 10 percent, under the 1967 amendments to the Social Security Act.[4] Such deductions thus tax quite heavily the earnings of the working poor, and the argument that the funds are used to finance benefits for the nonworking poor is not persuasive.

Alternatively, financing higher benefits from general revenues achieves some redistribution of income from high to low incomes,

3. The degree of regressiveness, however, is subject to debate. See Robert J. Myers, "Employee Social Insurance Contributions and Regressive Taxation," *Journal of Risk and Insurance,* 34 (December, 1967), 611–615. For a reexamination of social security policies, and an analysis of alternative arrangements for financing retirement income, see Joseph A. Pechman, Henry Aaron, and Michael K. Taussig, *Social Security: Perspectives for Reform* (Washington: Brookings Institution, 1968).

4. There is some disagreement as to the incidence of the employer's portion of the payroll tax. See the Social Security Administration's statement on this point in *Hearings before the House Committee on Ways and Means,* 90th Congress, 1st session, March, 1967, Part I, pp. 330–331; and the criticism of this position by John A. Brittain, "The Real Rate of Interest on Lifetime Contributions toward Retirement under Social Security," Joint Economic Committee, *Old Age Income Assurance,* Part III, 90th Congress, 1st session, 1968, pp. 109–132.

since the primary sources of federal revenues are the progressive personal and corporate income taxes. The greater the reliance on general revenues, therefore, the greater the redistributive effect; proposals that all benefits be financed in this manner have been offered. A more frequent recommendation has been to finance only a portion of the costs—one-third for example—from general revenues.

In the congressional hearings on the 1967 revisions of the social security system,[5] Colin D. Campbell proposed that the payroll tax be fixed at a rate that would allow new persons coming under coverage to receive in benefits during their retirement the amount of their own contributions and those made by their employers. The tax rate required to finance the new entrant's benefit would be lower than the present combined contribution; Campbell estimates 5.4 percent, or 2.7 percent each on employer and employee, which is almost two-thirds of the level-cost rate. The remaining costs—all benefits, that is, that are paid to present retirees in excess of what they paid for—should come from general revenues. Measures to improve income levels of retirees, such as increases in minimum benefits, or benefit increases commensurate with the rise in median family income, would also be financed from general revenues "whenever they increase the benefits of persons without at the same time increasing their tax contributions."[6]

Estimates of the tax rate necessary to pay for any specified level of benefits must take into account the probable rise in earnings during the lifetime of the worker. As taxable earnings increase, the level of benefits that can be supported also increases. John A. Brittain[7] has demonstrated that the rise in real incomes makes it possible for retirees to receive more in benefits than they and their employers paid in taxes; a real rate of interest of about 4 percent can be earned by the average participant, under the growth conditions prevailing in recent years. This real rate of interest is the sum of the rates of growth of per capita wages and population, as Henry Aaron[8] showed in an

---

5. *Hearings before the House Committee on Ways and Means*, 90th Congress, 1st session, March, 1967, Parts I, II, III, and IV. See also a summary and analysis of the financing issues by Dorothy S. Projector, "Should the Payroll Tax Finance Higher Benefits under OASDI?" *Journal of Human Resources*, 4 (1969), 60–75.

6. *Hearings before the House Committee on Ways and Means*, 90th Congress, 1st session, March, 1967, Part III, p. 1390.

7. "The Real Rate of Interest on Lifetime Contributions toward Retirement under Social Security," pp. 109–132.

8. "The Social Insurance Paradox," Joint Economic Committee, *Old Age Income Assurance*, Part V, pp. 15–18.

extension of the earlier "social insurance paradox" set forth by Paul A. Samuelson.[9] The "average" return of 4 percent which Brittain derives is not applicable to the contributions of wage earners at all levels. Because of the progressive quality of the benefit, the return to contributors with low earnings is higher than that made to high-wage earners.[10]

But even the somewhat higher return to low-income workers is not a valid basis for exacting a portion of that income in taxes, Brittain argues. The poor must borrow at very high interest rates (36 percent or more), meanwhile being forced to save for a return of 6 to 7 percent.

> A 6 or 7 percent ultimate real yield on the 10 percent contribution paid by the young $2,500 earner may sound attractive to some policymakers, but who would presume to call this worker a profligate glutton if he would rather have the 10 percent *now?* [11]

In a summary of the issues involved in the tax-benefit ratio, Dorothy Projector emphasizes the major dilemma: for many families, adequate income in old age can be afforded only at the expense of adequate income during youth.[12]

WHAT ARE THE FUNCTIONS OF OASDI?

Measures to improve the income levels of the aged are defended on different bases: present incomes are low relative to some index of minimum adequacy—the Orshansky poor or near-poor level, for example; or the aged's incomes are low relative to their own preretirement incomes; or they are low relative to the incomes of younger persons and families who are still at work. In any program designed to raise incomes in old age, the role of federal old-age insurance is clearly central. Yet it is important to ask whether we should rely altogether on social security benefits as a means of establishing an adequate minimum income for each retiree, regardless of his past contributions, or whether some minimum income should be provided to all families through a program financed from general revenues. In the latter case,

---

9. "An Exact Consumption-Loan Model of Interest with or without the Social Contrivance of Money," *Journal of Political Economy*, 66 (1958), 467–482.

10. Brittain, "The Real Rate of Interest on Lifetime Contributions toward Retirement under Social Security," pp. 124–125.

11. Ibid., p. 130.

12. "Should the Payroll Tax Finance Higher Benefits under OASDI?" p. 73.

wage-related benefits could then be paid to retirees as an addition to the guaranteed income, from the funds collected in payroll taxes.

Criticism of the OASDI system on the grounds that it is an inefficient way to reduce poverty is frequently voiced. The President's National Advisory Commission on Rural Poverty commented that little if any increased OASDI benefit would go to the poor—less than one-fifth, if benefits were raised by 20 percent. Moreover, the commission indicated that

> under the benefit formulas used, if OASDI payments were increased by 50 percent rather than 20 percent, the poor would get an even smaller percentage of the benefits. This is so because benefits are paid to those who are not poor as well as to those who are poor, and each increase in incomes means that a larger percentage of the benefits goes to those who are not poor.[13]

In a similar vein, Dorothy Projector points out that an expenditure in the form of welfare payments or negative tax supplements would remove more families from poverty than the same expenditure in OASDI benefits. She suggests that we "recognize that OASDI cannot solve all problems of income maintenance and . . . move in the direction of creating additional mechanisms for meeting the need for further redistribution of income."[14]

Proposals for providing a universal pension to all elderly persons have been made repeatedly. Eveline Burns has long advocated a double-decker system of payments, in which a demogrant (a uniform payment to all persons at some specified age) would be supplemented by a wage-related benefit.[15] The former would be financed from general revenues, the latter from payroll taxes. Margaret Gordon has also proposed a flat pension for persons aged 65 and over (or failing this, for all those aged 70 or more), and income-conditioned benefits in addition.[16] The widespread use of such schemes in European countries is cited by both authors.

The alleviation of poverty in old age is perhaps best achieved

13. *The People Left Behind* (Washington: The President's National Advisory Commission on Rural Poverty, 1967), p. 87.

14. Projector, "Should the Payroll Tax Finance Higher Benefits under OASDI?" p. 74.

15. See her "Social Security in Evolution," *Social Service Review,* 39 (1965), 129–140; also, "Income-Maintenance Policies and Early Retirement," in Kreps, *Technology, Manpower, and Retirement Policy,* pp. 125–140.

16. Margaret S. Gordon, "The Case for Earnings-Related Social Security Benefits Restated," Joint Economic Committee, *Old Age Income Assurance,* Part II, pp. 312–339.

through a universal pension, leaving to social insurance the function generally assigned to it, that is, the replacement during retirement of some portion of previous earnings. Separation of the two components of the aged's income would permit the establishment of some minimum income for all aged persons, regardless of their previous earnings records, while also preserving the present structure of OASDI benefits and contributions. In her argument for such a scheme, Margaret Gordon points out that a pension of $50 for individuals and $75 for couples aged 65 or over would mean that those now receiving minimum benefits would receive approximately $100 a month (individuals) and $150 a month (couples), or $1,200 and $1,800 annually. These minima would bring the couples almost up to Orshansky's nonfarm poverty line of $1,850, and would move the individuals much closer to their poverty level of $1,435. Aged individuals and couples now receiving average OASDI benefits, moreover, would have their incomes raised almost to Orshansky's nonfarm low-income levels for the elderly. The net costs of a universal pension of this amount are difficult to estimate because of offsetting savings; the annual costs before such savings are deducted would be about $9.9 billion.[17]

If the problem of extreme poverty in old age were to be met by a guarantee of income, either to the elderly or to all persons, it would then be possible to concentrate attention on improving the ratio of pension income to earnings. This ratio is extremely low, and projections indicate that

> U.S. pension systems, as they are presently developing, are failing to generate for large numbers of aged persons retirement income sufficient to meet generally accepted international and national standards of pension-earnings ratio adequacy.[18]

The earnings-replacement function of OASDI has sometimes been overlooked in the rash of proposals for alleviating poverty.

FINANCIAL AND REAL SUPPORT OF NONWORKERS

Many differences of view as to the financing of OASDI benefits arise from difficulties inherent in imputing to the system the responsibility for achieving both individual equity and socially defined adequacy.

17. Ibid., p. 336.
18. James H. Schulz, "Aged Retirement Income Adequacy: Simulation Projections of Pension-Earnings Ratios," p. 259.

Individual equity means that the contributor receives benefit protection directly related to the amount of his contributions— or, in other words, actuarially equivalent thereto. Social adequacy means that the benefits paid will provide for all contributors a certain standard of living.[19]

A social insurance scheme which provides only individual equity, by Myers's definition, achieves a temporal reapportionment of a family's income. But redistribution of income between income classes occurs only to the extent that some goal of social equity is sought—a goal which specifies certain minimum incomes, for example, regardless of previous earnings records. Under OASDI provisions, retirement benefits are only remotely related to previous earnings; still, the rationale that benefits accrue because one pays into the system is apparently important to both workers and retirees.

The redistributive effect of old-age insurance programs, examined in a recent study by Benjamin Bridges,[20] will continue to be both applauded and viewed with alarm. But the impact of recent demographic and technological changes on patterns of income distribution apply to the young as well as the old; for both groups, the trends would seem to indicate greater support from transfers and less from earnings. Two of the key questions would seem to be: what are the social forces bringing about the greater transfers of income to non-working groups; and to what extent and in what form will the transfers grow? The latter question seems to be particularly critical, in view of the current drive to improve the educational and skill levels of youth and minority groups, and workers only marginally attached to the labor force.[21]

Of the many factors involved in the growth of income maintenance for persons not at work, one broad development—the rise in productivity per manhour—is of particular significance. Increases in productivity, in fact, might be credited in large measure with both originating the need for income transfers (by requiring a more highly educated labor force, by increasing the pressure for retirement as less labor per unit of output is required, by increasing unemployment, at least in the short run, and so forth) and providing the means of meeting this need, that is, an increased total product. Needless to say, an

19. Robert J. Myers, *Social Insurance and Allied Government Programs* (Homewood, Ill.: Richard D. Irwin, 1965) , p. 6.

20. "Current Redistributional Effects of Old-Age Income Assurance Programs," Joint Economic Committee, *Old Age Income Assurance,* Part II, pp. 95–176.

21. For further discussion, see Kreps, "The Economics of Intergenerational Relationships," pp. 279–287.

increased capacity to support nonworking groups does not mean that society chooses to allocate its output in such a manner. Conceivably, larger volumes of goods could continue to be distributed functionally, leaving nonworking persons and their families dependent upon private charity, savings, support by relatives, and the like. In the United States, the initial decision to allocate a portion of the nation's output to persons not currently at work was actually made at a point in the nation's history when the total output was extremely low, and when the major economic problem—unemployment—sprang not from any sudden or sharp rises in productivity but from financial collapse and the ensuing decline in aggregate demand for goods. Thus significant transfers of income originated in a situation in which rising productivity played no immediate role.

Since the end of World War II, increases in productivity have been a major concern throughout the world. In the United States the desire for a higher rate of economic growth (and a faster rise in productivity) has been fed by the knowledge that many other nations were enjoying growth rates considerably in excess of ours. Yet the productivity trends in this country have been impressive. This increase in output per manhour, enabling the economy to produce larger and larger volumes of goods with little or no expansion in the number of manhours required, is precisely what gives rise to the argument that increases in productivity in fact create the need for transfers of income. Inevitably, the short-run problem of technological unemployment arises, making it necessary to provide temporary income for disemployed workers and their families. But longer-run considerations are involved in financing intergenerational shifts in income. In the case both of providing retirement income and providing income maintenance during a lengthened period of education, several years' income is in question. Moreover, the particular employment problems of the very young worker in recent years have made it quite clear that the alternative to increased expenditures for education is increased expenditures for unemployment compensation.

Given present trends toward lengthening the period of education and reducing the work activity of older men, it is not unlikely that the number of years a man spends outside the labor force could increase significantly during the decades of the 1970s. For example, suppose that the average age of full-time entry to the labor force rose by two years while the retirement age dropped by two years. A man would then have an additional four years in which he would be supported by nonwage income. In addition, it seems likely that most new increases in life expectancy will be added to the number of years spent outside the labor force. The former division of any extra years of life between working and not working will change, as job opportunities, particularly for older men, diminish.

Yet since output is increasing without any substantial increase in manhours worked, it is clear that a man can expect his lifetime output to remain at least at its present level, even if his worklife span declines, or his total manhours of work decline through a shortened workweek. In essence, the man who in the future will work from age 20 to age 60 will produce at least as much as the man who in an earlier period worked from age 18 to age 65. Very likely, the output of the man with the shorter worklife will be greater, particularly if it can be supposed that his health is better than that of the worker of earlier generations, and if the number of years he is forced to spend in involuntary unemployment is at least not increased.

If a man's total output is in fact rising, even though he is spending an increasing number of adult years outside the labor force, the problem of supporting him and his family through a lengthened educational period and a lengthened retirement period can be viewed in part as a problem of spreading total earnings through the lifespan, rather than concentrating them during the working years. A partial evening-out of the income stream need not, of course, provide the same income for each year of adult life. In fact, given the changing pattern of financial needs and expenditures through the family cycle —education, marriage, birth of first child, support of older children, the husband-and-wife family in which at least the head is still at work, and finally, the retirement period for two, and then one person—the annual income ideally would vary in accordance with changing needs. Nevertheless, it becomes increasingly important that the life earnings of husband and wife be viewed in the perspective of their lifetime needs and that those earnings be spread somewhat more evenly through adult life, rather than being concentrated within the years of actual labor force activity.

For the individual family, savings, the acquisition of a private pension claim, and the building up of equity in a home are the most frequent examples of deferred consumption during relatively high-income years in return for money or real income during retirement. The family which envisions its long-range as well as its short-run finanical needs and budgets its expenditures and savings accordingly is thus evening-out its income in one direction, at least. In so doing, the family is merely extending a budgeting principle applied monthly by many families whose income is not received in twelve equal installments, but who divide their annual total income by twelve and then regulate their expenditures in accordance with this average.

At the aggregate level, a society's capacity to support adults for longer periods of education and in retirement depends upon that society's capacity to produce. The productive potential of the American economy, which is expected to make ever greater strides under the continued technological thrust of the era, is clearly capable of rendering an output sufficiently large to provide for its members both an adequate supply of goods and an increased number of years free of work. Shifts in the pattern of distribution which enable nonworking adults and their families to share in the national product, principally typified up to now by the OASDI program, may gradually be extended on a much broader scale to young nonworking adults and their families.

14. THE SEPARATION OF WORK AND INCOME *

One of the things we know for certain about any age group is that it has no future. The young become middle-aged and the middle-aged become old, and the old die. Consequently, the support which the middle-aged give to the young can be regarded as the first part of a deferred exchange, which will be consummated when those who are now young become middle-aged and support those who are now middle-aged who will then be old. Similarly, the support which the middle-aged give to the old can be regarded as the consummation of a bargain entered into a generation ago.[1]

The transfer of income between generations, now made primarily through governmental agencies rather than family units, has come to be accepted as a concomitant of the lengthened lifespan prevailing in advanced countries throughout the world. A rationale for such intergenerational support can easily be deduced, as Boulding's comment demonstrates.

Public transfers of income to families headed by persons of working age have been provided only under certain circumstances, however. Unemployment insurance and cash benefits to the disabled worker have been the only major sources of public support for males of work-

* In an earlier article, "Separation of Work and Income," in Frances F. Korten et al., *Psychology and the Problems of Society* (Washington: American Psychological Association, 1970), pp. 140–151, the author discusses the issue in the broader context of income guarantees for all groups.

1. Kenneth E. Boulding, "Reflections on Poverty," *The Social Welfare Forum: 1961* (New York: Columbia University Press, 1961), pp. 45–58; reprinted in Herman P. Miller, *Poverty American Style* (Belmont, Calif.: Wadsworth, 1968), pp. 42–51.

ing age, with aid to dependent children being generally restricted to families without male heads, until very recently. Unemployment and disability payments, financed by payroll taxes, are viewed as a form of insurance, and hence are available only to workers who have made contributions, or have had employers who contributed. Thus the male of working age has been eligible for a public transfer only by reason of his attachment to the labor force.

INCOME WITHOUT WORK: THE RATIONALE

How, then, have we come to the present stage of discussion of a guaranteed income for all? Is the emergence of new approaches to income maintenance due to a recognition of defects in the existing system? Or is the output of the economy now so large that the nation can "afford" to offer some minimum family income? To what extent does the widespread endorsement of such schemes as the negative income tax, which would be available without reference to employment, belie a belief that work is no longer necessary?

The workless society has been promised from time to time, usually on the basis that automation will soon eliminate the need for human labor. Robert Theobald, the widely quoted author of *Free Men and Free Markets*, maintains that "the guaranteed income is a philosophical principle which argues that every man is entitled to a minimum income at a time when machines can produce enough for all." Moreover,

> provision of income as a right will bring us to understand that money itself is an anachronism in a cybernated era. Money was needed to ration scarce goods and industrial services in the past, but it is a highly unsatisfactory means of determining priorities in a cybernated era. Society will find it more satisfactory, in terms of scarce resources, to distribute many types of goods and services without money payments.[2]

A constitutionally guaranteed income, he argues, is essential in an era when human labor is no longer necessary to the production of goods. But the fact that "man has a pathological desire to toil" means that he will not remain idle but will turn his attention to those pursuits that interest him, once his basic needs are assured. By eliminat-

2. "The Guaranteed Income in Perspective," in Thomas A. Naylor, ed., *The Impact of the Computer on Society* (Atlanta: Southern Regional Education Board, 1966), pp. 64, 71.

ing money as a means of motivation, he concludes, people will do those things that make the best use of their talents.

Although few economists have agreed with Theobald that work was on its way out, technology's role in the development and persistence of high levels of unemployment during the 1950s and early 1960s has been the subject of some concern. Statistics showing that the number of jobs grows each year, despite the inroads of automation, are not completely reassuring; the question is not whether employment increases but whether unemployment increases. And during most of the two decades following World War II, the level of unemployment has been high, ranging from 7 percent to 5 percent. Only with the Vietnamese war did the rate fall below 4 percent.

Unemployment of such magnitudes in an era of prosperity and rising incomes and prices inevitably lends support to arguments for guaranteed family incomes. Whether the unemployment is an outgrowth of technological change or a result of lagging economic growth, the problem of providing income to the unemployed remains much the same. The National Commission on Technology concluded in 1966 that income-maintenance arrangements needed to be reexamined, not because automation made human labor obsolete, but because we could afford to guarantee incomes to all persons.

> We are convinced that rising productivity has brought this country to the point at last when all citizens may have a decent standard of living at a cost in resources the economy can easily bear . . . the road to satisfying life through work is not open to everyone: not to families without breadwinners, not to those whose productivity is reduced by physical or mental incapacity, not to people too old to work. . . .
>
> The Commission recommends that Congress go beyond a reform of the present structure and examine wholly new approaches to the problem of income maintenance. In particular, we suggest that Congress give serious study to a "minimum income allowance" or "negative income tax" program. Such a program, if found feasible, would be designed to approach by stages the goal of eliminating the need for means test public assistance programs by providing a floor of adequate minimum incomes.[3]

Thus, not out of fear of technology but because, as a gift of technology, the economy could afford to do so, the commission proposed

3. *Technology and the American Economy*, Report of the National Commission on Technology, Automation, and Economic Progress, Washington, 1966, p. 38.

minimum guaranteed incomes; "to say don't worry about automation and computers as a cause of unemployment is not to say don't worry." [4] Moreover, the problem of low incomes extends to families whose heads are employed. Mollie Orshansky estimated that in 1966 one-fourth of all poor families were headed by men who had worked throughout the year; among poor families headed by men under age 65, five out of six of the heads worked some time during the year.[5] Supplements to the earnings of these workers are clearly a necessary part of any scheme designed to alleviate poverty.

INCOME WITHOUT WORK: THE SCHEMES

In a recent discussion of income transfer programs, Henry J. Aaron identifies three groups of poor: one, the employed and employable (working age males and working age females without children) ; two, those for whom employment is not feasible (the aged, the disabled, and the blind) ; and three, mothers of working age, for whom jobs may or may not be available and appropriate. Income maintenance programs aim to replace income losses incurred primarily by the second group, who have suffered death of the breadwinner, retirement from work, disability, or some other termination or interruption of earnings. Income supplements, on the other hand, are provided because incomes are recognized as inadequate and are made without reference to any previous earnings records.[6]

Systems of transfers aimed at restoring income, in particular, the OASDI benefits, can of course be made to serve the poor aged to a greater degree than they now do. Aaron suggests (in addition to the removal of payroll taxes on the poor) that the scheme be reformed to increase the benefits of aged single persons, whose incomes are lower than those of elderly couples; to raise minimum benefits; to eliminate the practice of paying benefits to early retirees. Alternatively, as Burns has suggested, the payment of a demogrant to all aged persons, plus a wage-related benefit which restores some portion of previous earnings, would serve the poor without disturbing the present structure of social security payments.

4. Garth L. Mangum, "The Computer in the American Economy," in Naylor, *The Impact of the Computer on Society*, p. 98.

5. Mollie Orshansky, "The Shape of Poverty in 1966," *Social Security Bulletin*, 31 (March, 1968) , 14–15.

6. "Income Transfer Programs," *Monthly Labor Review*, 92 (February, 1969) , 50–54.

Reforms in the present system of welfare payments are currently under discussion, in part because of obvious defects, and in part because of the appearance of alternative proposals for guaranteeing minimum incomes. It is generally recognized that the public assistance programs as now run by the various states fail to meet the needs of the 35 million poor. Coverage is restricted, earnings are discouraged, desertion of families is encouraged. Average benefits vary widely among the states: from a monthly $8.45 per person in Mississippi to $68.55 in New York.

Negative Income Tax Proposals

One of the earliest proponents of an alternative plan was Milton Friedman, who in *Capitalism and Freedom* proposed a simple negative income tax arrangement to replace the present proliferation of public assistance and government welfare programs. Friedman's plan would apply a tax rate of, say, 50 percent to a family's unused exemptions and minimum standard deductions. If the minimum standard deductions for a family of five were $3,700, and their income $2,000, unused exemptions and deductions would be $1,700. Fifty percent of this amount, or $850, would raise the family income to $2,850. The effective minimum income in this case would be $1,850, which would be the maximum payment going to a family with no other income.

Numerous variations on this theme have been composed. They involve a symmetrizing of the present income tax structure, with payments being made by the Internal Revenue Service, upon the receipt of a statement of income similar to an ordinary tax form. They are noncategorical in coverage. Eligibility (in most proposals, based on the family as a unit) would be determined solely by income and family size; consequently, the problems of determining eligibility in exclusionary categories would be eliminated.

Although many variations have been suggested, they all require decisions on the base to which the rate is to be applied, the tax rate, the effective minimum, and a break-even point. Two possible *bases* have been under consideration: (*a*) the unused exemptions and minimum standard deductions of a family with no taxable income and (*b*) the poverty-income gap, which is the difference between an officially established poverty line for a particular size family and that family's money income. Although the two bases differ substantially only for very small or very large families, the poverty-income gap is generally considered a better indicator of need.

As to *tax rate,* it should be noted that the present public assistance system operates under what amounts to a 100 percent tax—for every dollar earned, the public assistance allotment is reduced by a dollar. This provides a disincentive to work. The negative income tax attempts to provide some work incentive by allowing the poor to keep a percentage of their earnings in addition to the payment. This means a tax rate considerably lower than 100 percent. Not only does a 100 percent rate eliminate the monetary incentive to work; it could result in a much greater cost to the economy.

The *effective minimum income* can be either a stated floor or simply the amount paid on a particular scale to a family with zero income. The *break-even point* is that point at which a family's tax liability equals its guaranteed income, and thus the payment becomes zero.

While endorsing the principle of negative income taxation, Robert Lampman has viewed the scheme as a supplement to other welfare programs. Public assistance payments should be greatly reduced by negative taxes under his proposals, but he would not eliminate OASDHI benefits, for example.[7] In one of his plans he suggested a $750 allowance for families with incomes up to $1,500, with a reduction of 50 percent in the allowance for any income over $1,500. In this manner, he would provide some work incentive for low-income workers. But since the benefits are clearly inadequate for families with the lowest incomes, the scheme relies on public assistance to supplement the allowance. Another of his earlier plans called for an effective minimum of $1,500, with the poverty-income level of $3,000 for a family of four, and negative tax rates that vary inversely with the income. If the family's income is $500, their poverty-income gap is $2,500, and payment at 45 percent of the gap would add $1,125, for a total income of $1,625. For a family with a $2,000 income, payment at 25 percent of the gap would add $250 to the income. This plan concentrated its benefits on the poorest of the poor but, like all negative income tax plans, was designed to reach many people who were working and not on relief, yet whose incomes were considered inadequate by today's standard.

James Tobin would have an income guarantee high enough to raise those families with no other income out of poverty, and a tax rate low enough to provide incentives for those who can work. For example, if the guarantee were to equal the $3,000 poverty line for a family of four, and the tax rate set at 50 percent, a family with an income of $2,000 would receive $2,000 ($3,000 less 50 percent of

7. "Approaches to the Reduction of Poverty," *American Economic Review, Papers and Proceedings*, 55 (May, 1965), 521–529. Also, see his "Programs for Poverty," *Proceedings of the 57th Annual Conference of the National Tax Association*, Pittsburgh, September, 1964, pp. 71–81.

their previous income), making their total income $4,000. He has pointed out that if the income guarantee is to be sufficient to support a family, and yet provide an incentive to work, it is impossible to avoid making payments to families who are above the poverty line. (In the example given above, the break-even point would be an income of $6,000.) [8]

This can be avoided in any plan which provides a reasonable income floor and less than a 100 percent rate, but only at the cost of producing what has been called the "notch" effect. If a minimum of $3,000, for instance, is specified, with a tax rate of 50 percent, and families with incomes over $3,000 are excluded, a family with a $2,000 income would receive $2,000 ($3,000 less 50 percent of $2,000), making their total income $4,000. This would be more than that of a family whose own earnings of $3,500 prohibited them from receiving any assistance. The logical thing for the second family to do would be to curtail its earnings until they dropped below the $3,000 level.

In his review of these and other negative income tax plans, Christopher Green argues that the schemes represent an attack on poverty with a minimum of income redistribution; further, that the plans allow the poor to benefit from tax cuts, where the cuts include an increase in the negative rate. Tax reductions at present do not benefit the poor directly, whether the tax rate is being reduced or the level of personal exemptions and deductions is being raised.[9] With Lampman, he emphasizes the fact that guaranteed incomes are not a substitute for long-range programs designed to increase labor productivity: "It is not inconsistent to provide money income for the poor and at the same time make government expenditures for ràising the productivity of the poor." [10]

Problems and Alternatives

The negative income tax shares with other guaranteed income plans an essential component: it involves a direct transfer of money to the poor. Consequently, the tax schemes face the same initial problem as other plans offering this guarantee, namely that of avoiding payments to the nonpoor, while at the same time making the guarantee adequate and avoiding the disincentive characteristic of public assistance programs.

Several alternatives to the negative income tax have been proposed;

8. James Tobin, "Improving the Economic Status of the Negro," *Daedalus,* 94 (Fall, 1965), 889–895.
9. Christopher Green, *Negative Taxes and the Poverty Problem* (Washington: Brookings Institution, 1967), p. 61.
10. Ibid., pp. 8–9.

revision of the public assistance system is one suggestion. Benefits and coverage should be expanded, additional public services provided, and the means test simplified. The poor are not a homogeneous group, the argument runs, and a single program cannot be expected to meet the needs of all. Earlier, the Advisory Council on Public Welfare suggested a revision of the public assistance system which would have turned it into a form of guaranteed income plan. The federal government would have established an income floor and provided the states with all the necessary funds, eligibility for payments to be determined entirely by the family's needs.

A comprehensive review of the income levels and needs of the poor emerged as the findings of the President's Commission on Income Maintenance Programs. In its réport published in late 1969, the commission recommended "the creation of a universal income supplement program financed and administered by Federal Government, making cash payments to all members of the population with income needs." [11] Specifically, an income of $2,400 for a family of four was proposed, with this basic payment being reduced by fifty cents for each dollar of other income. Thus a family of this size would receive some income subsidy up to a level of $4,800, when supplementation would cease. Recognizing that the prescribed minimum income was below the commonly used poverty line, the commission urged that the minimum be raised as rapidly as possible; to specify incomes at the poverty line, according to their estimate, would cost about $27 billion.

These recommendations came from a body appointed by President Johnson. In the meantime, President Nixon's proposal for a system of guaranteed income had appeared, requesting a minimum of $1,600 for a family of four. His scheme also attempted to take account of the wage incentive issue by allowing earnings of as much as $720 before any reduction in governmental payment occurred. Beyond $720, each dollar of earnings reduced the income subsidy by fifty cents, up to a total income of $3,920. In order to receive the payment, heads of household would be required to take jobs or enroll in job training programs, unless the household head were the mother of preschool children.[12]

Neither the $2,400 nor the $1,600 minimum has been put into effect. Nor would serious congressional consideration of these proposals

11. *Poverty Amid Plenty: The American Paradox*, Report of the President's Commission on Income Maintenance Programs (Washington: Government Printing Office, 1969), p. 7.
12. "Toward a Full Opportunity for Every American: The President's Proposals for Welfare Reform," *Welfare in Review*, 7 (September–October, 1969), 1–11.

appear to be forthcoming until the fiscal problems generated by military spending and overall inflationary pressures are eased. The issue of a guaranteed minimum income will nevertheless persist, and attention will revert to these recommendations in time. It is clear that there is now widespread public support for some form of minimum income, despite continued debate on the question of how closely this income should be tied to work. At least three issues are relevant to the debate: costs (in terms of alternative programs) ; incentives, and their role in determining total output; and questions of equity.

INCOME WITHOUT WORK: THE ISSUES

Negative income taxation has been classified as a watered-down version of social dividend transaction, which in turn is defined as a

> tax-transfer system in which every family begins the year with an income guarantee. . . . The essence of social dividend taxation is that it combines negative and positive taxes in such a way as to build a floor under the income of every family. It requires the tax system to raise revenues to finance the guaranteed minimum income to everybody as well as to finance other public services.[13]

The Question of Costs

The immediate objection raised to any scheme of guaranteed income is that of the cost involved. Cost estimates vary, depending largely on the size of the individual or family allowance. James Tobin's plan for a basic annual allowance of $400 per person, with an upper limit of $2,700 per family, was estimated to cost about $14 billion, based on 1962 income data.[14] In the early days of the antipoverty program, the Council of Economic Advisers' figure of $11 billion was widely cited as the cost of raising families to a $3,000 and individuals to a $1,500 minimum. Translated into alternative uses, $11 billion amounted to about one-fifth of the annual defense budget and less than 2 percent of the gross national product. The President's Commission on Income Maintenance estimated a cost of $27 billion to bring all incomes up to the poverty level.

When the economy's output is growing and tax revenues are rising (even without increases in tax rates), aggregate costs of these mag-

13. Green, *Negative Taxes and the Poverty Problem*, p. 54.
14. "Improving the Economic Status of the Negro."

nitudes do not appear prohibitive. But an expenditure on any program can be judged as appropriate only when its advantages outweigh those accruing from a similar expenditure on some alternative program. A majority view would probably hold in favor of income supplements over military spending, space exploration, and very likely, over foreign aid. But these budget items do not exhaust the list of possible priorities. What of an alternative expenditure to provide medical and dental care to low-income families? Would improved educational facilities make a more significant long-run contribution to the elimination of poverty? Rather than offer the income directly, would the provision for certain basic needs (housing, food, health care) at public expense be a better use of the funds? Extending the range of social goals to other possible priorities, we find that

> we could rebuild all our cities or abolish poverty; or replace all the obsolete plant and equipment in private industry; or we could . . . develop the hardware to get us to Mars and back before the year 2000. We could make some progress on all the goals, perhaps substantial progress on many, but we cannot accomplish all our aspirations at the same time.[15]

The question of costs is further complicated by the role of wage incentives. Will the guarantee of some minimum income reduce the amount of effort devoted to work, thereby reducing total output? To the extent that this reduction occurs, the cost of the income-supplement program is higher than the dollar cost of providing the allowance; it must include also the cost of the foregone output. Clearly, one's appraisal of the extent of our reliance on income as a motivating force in getting work done conditions his estimate of the true costs of income guarantees. Moreover, since income supplements must be paid for with tax revenues, one must reckon with a potential reduction in work effort on the part of the group whose incomes are being taxed to finance the allowances.

The Question of Incentives

The disincentive effect of income taxes has been exaggerated, according to George F. Break. From interviews with accountants and solicitors who were subject to high marginal and average tax rates (and who could control their work hours), he found the following attitude: "When you get right down to it, I am working as hard as I

15. Leonard Lecht, *The Dollar Cost of Our National Goals* (Washington: National Planning Association, 1965), p. 5.

ever worked. I complain bitterly about how little I am allowed to keep of every pound I earn, but I go on working just the same." [16]

The author notes that several factors will tend to cause workers to offer the same amount of labor, despite the imposition of income taxes: the tendency toward larger families, which increases commitments; higher divorce rates; increasing demand for consumer durables; the entrance of wives to the labor force, notwithstanding higher marginal tax rates; greater domestic and foreign travel which stimulates demand; greater urbanization, with the "bandwagon" effect on consumption patterns; decreasing flexibility of the individual's working habits, which reduces the individual's propensity to change his working hours in response to a tax increase.

The question whether the members of low-income families would work less if they no longer had to rely on earnings to provide the basic necessities is difficult to subject to empirical test.[17] The threat that certain jobs—the less pleasant, and generally lowest-paying ones —would not get done continues in many quarters to argue against income guarantees for the male of working age. Even though such jobs would presumably enable the family to achieve a level of living above the minimum standard, there persists some skepticism that the availability of additional income would provide adequate work incentive, if a subsistence level of living is assured.

Conflicting views are currently being expressed as to the effect of public income subsidies on the supply of labor. Lowell Gallaway questions the contribution a negative income tax plan would make to the income of the poor, except for those poor whose labor force activity is quite limited; it is possible, he suggests, that the receipt of a transfer actually lowers a family's income, by reducing work effort and lowering earnings.[18] Brehm and Saving, investigating the impact of general assistance payments, conclude that there are higher proportions of the population receiving payments in the states with higher average levels of GAP transfers. By implication, work is more often withheld in order to receive the welfare check, when the check is larger.[19] Kasper's study contradicts these findings, however. He

16. "Income Taxes and Incentives to Work: An Empirical Study," *American Economic Review*, 47 (September, 1957), 548.

17. See Martin David and Roger F. Miller, "The Work Leisure Choice under a Tax and Transfer Regime" (Madison: University of Wisconsin, Social Systems Research Institute, 1968), mimeographed.

18. "Negative Income Tax and the Elimination of Poverty," *National Tax Journal*, 19 (September, 1966), 298–307.

19. C. T. Brehm and T. R. Saving, "The Demand for General Assistance Payments," *American Economic Review*, 54 (December, 1964), 1002–1018.

argues that differences in labor market conditions, not differences in the level of welfare payments, are primarily responsible for interstate variation in the proportion of people drawing general assistance.[20] Two other models again present diverse conclusions. Leuthold finds that on the average, work effort increases somewhat for the population as a whole, in response to the introduction of a formula transfer program.[21] Perlman, in the same issue of the same journal, notes that in using a negative tax

> the only possibility for maintaining labor supply would come about through a technique of making the marginal income received greater than the amount earned without a negative tax. This would require not only that the subsidy be graduated, but graduated in such a way that the extra amount received would increase with the number of hours worked near the full schedule for these workers receiving a subsidy.[22]

Except in some such plan as the one Perlman describes, it is generally thought that some work effort will be sacrificed in a program of subsidies to low income families. Christopher Green, one spokesman for a negative income tax, summarizes the usual reasoning of the economist:

> If both income and leisure are "normal" goods, and if preference patterns are not changed as a result of implementation of a negative income tax plan, utility maximizing individuals will choose to work less in the presence of negative tax payments than in their absence. How much less depends on the level of the income guarantee, the negative (marginal) tax rate, and the shape of the utility function.[23]

Questions of Equity

Programs which might discourage work are seen as deterrents to a high rate of growth in output. Threats to the *size* of the nation's output are only one part of the objection, however; even stronger protests are heard because of the possible impact on the *distribution* of

20. Hirschel Kasper, "Welfare Payments and Work Incentive: Some Determinants of the Rates of General Assistance Payments," *Journal of Human Resources,* 3 (Winter, 1968), 86–110.

21. Jane H. Leuthold, "An Empirical Study of Formula Income Transfers and the Work Decision of the Poor," *Journal of Human Resources,* 3 (Summer, 1968), 312–323.

22. Richard Perlman, "A Negative Income Tax Plan for Maintaining Incentives," ibid., pp. 298–299.

23. Christopher Green, "Negative Taxes and Monetary Incentives to Work: The Static Theory," ibid., p. 280.

that output. In general, the distribution scheme espoused for our economy has been one which confers income in accordance with productivity. Such a reward system is found acceptable because it is thought to be fair—"a man gets what he is worth and he is worth what he gets." Leaving aside the difficulties of measurement, which might provide evidence whether productivity does in fact determine wages, equity under this distributive scheme is frequently challenged on the basis that inadequate educational opportunities limit the productivity, and hence the earnings, of certain groups. Expenditures made for the purpose of improving educational opportunities are thus generally acceptable, since they enable the citizenry to be self-supporting.

The idea of using public funds to provide income, rather than the means of learning to earn income, is in many circles vehemently opposed, as long as there is any work alternative. The work ethic lends strong endorsement to present wage-employment arrangements, in which persons who receive income from public transfers are expected to be old or disabled. Any scheme which appears to be rewarding idleness by guaranteeing a minimum income is thus opposed by many, who think of income as a reward for effort. In short, equity arguments against minimum income guarantees are similar to the protests against income redistribution in general: the receipt of earnings is prima facie evidence that the income is in fact earned, or deserved. By implication, those without earnings are undeserving, and our reward system cannot confer pay on the undeserving.

SOME POINTS OF CONFLICT

There is a conflict of objectives in the negative income tax proposals, a German economist noted recently. The antipoverty schemes, aiming for greater equality of income, call for subsidies with negative tax rates such as those proposed in the United States. The more assistance given to the very poor, the faster these rates drop with a rise in income. But a work-incentive scheme, designed to increase the total product available to all, calls for rising subsidies with rising income, in the manner of the German system. Clearly, these payments discriminate against the poor. "We are left with the conclusion," he writes, "that the incentive and distributional objectives of the negative income tax plans are inherently contradictory." [24]

24. Klaus Peter Kisker, "A Note on the Negative Income Tax," *National Tax Journal,* 20 (March, 1967), 104.

We are caught in more than one contradiction, in fact. For one thing, we would like to guarantee a minimum income to all families regardless of current job status, and yet we are eager to preserve work incentives by making income depend on work. For another, we insist that the reward system pay for performance, which means it must penalize lack of performance if only by witholding payments, despite our recognition that human capabilities differ widely from one person to the next. Still a third set of problems arises from our ambivalence toward the meaning and role of work. In the best Puritan tradition, we claim that work is ennobling. But in all economic analysis, only income and leisure are desirable; the disutility of work is immediately recognized. Finally, we have given little thought to a possible substitute for pay, although there may be other, equally strong motivating forces that would serve the interests of the individual and society.

In the midst of these conflicting notions, we are reminded by one economist of the constraints that have always been imposed on any move to separate income from work. Programs to provide income in lieu of work "have been established on the conviction that they will promote the efficiency of the economy or at least will not make it less efficient." [25] Future measures, he predicts, will be subject to the same pragmatic test. If he is correct, it is difficult indeed to imagine any decisive move to sever income from work; we continue to reason that "pay is the most important single motivator used in our organized society.[26]

25. Valdemar Carlson, *Economic Security in the United States* (New York: McGraw-Hill, 1962), p. 214.
26. Marion Haire, Edwin S. Ghiselli, and Lyman W. Porter, "Psychological Research on Pay: An Overview," *Industrial Relations,* 3 (October, 1963), 3.

INDEX

Aaron, Henry J., 147, 158
Activity rates: changes in since 1950, 51–54; in the 1960s, 54–56
Advisory Council on Social Security, Old Age Assistance and, 39
Arena, John J., 102–103

Blackburn, John O., 134
Break, George F., 164–165
Brehm, C. T., 165
Bridges, Benjamin, 151
Brittain, John A., 147–148
Brumberg, Richard, 98–99
Burns, Eveline, 149, 158

Campbell, Colin D., 147
Clark, F. LeGros, 78
Consumption: patterns of, 16; factors determining level of, 24; affected by income growth, 98–99; reapportionment of, 100 ff.; models of time allocation of, 101 ff.; variants of, 113 ff.; expenditures of retired persons, 134; relation between expenditures of retired persons and workers, 135 ff.
Cost of living, 16

Demography, 39; unemployment and, 40
Distribution: of leisure, 40; of work, 40
Dubin, Robert, 19
Durand, John D., 65

Economic growth: alternative uses of, 77 ff.; and earnings, 88–93; and income, 133 ff.; and retirement income, 136 ff.; allocating gains from, 138 ff.
Expenditures, annual, 94–99; by occupation, 95; by age of family head, 95–96; compared with respective incomes, 96–98

Free time. See Leisure
Friedman, Milton, 102, 159

Gallaway, Lowell, 165
Garfinkle, Stuart, 48
Goldsmith, Raymond W., 98
Gordon, Margaret, 69 n., 149–150
Green, Christopher, 161, 166
Guaranteed minimum income, 156–168; schemes of, 158–161; and issue of costs, 163–164; and issue of incentives, 164–

166; and issue of equity, 166–167. See also Income

Income: discretionary, 4–5; distribution of, 13, 79; theory of allocation of, 13; determinants of, 13–14; guaranteed annual, 13, 156–168; redistribution of, 14; versus leisure, 23, 80 ff.; of the aged, 27 ff.; sources of during nonworking years, 27–32; of families classified by age of family head, Table 3.1, 29; theory of distribution, 34; relation to amount of work performed, 64 ff.; average hourly earnings, Table 6.1, 67; lifetime earnings, 81; by age and occupation, 85–93; estimates of retirement, 118 ff.
Income tax, negative. See Negative Income Tax
Income transfers: public, 155–156; programs of, 158–159. See also Transfer payments

Kasper, Hirschel, 165–166
Kuznets, Simon, 23

Labor participation rate, 41–49, 70. See also Labor force activity rates
Labor force activity rates, 41–49; by sex, 41; by age, 42 n., 43; by stage of industrialization, 42, 42 n., 43–44; in industrialized countries, 44
Lampman, Robert, 160
Leisure: allocation of, 14, 75; value of, 15–16; attitudes toward, 17–21; areas of, 20; growth and dimensions of, 21–22; distribution of, 26–27, 40–41; in the United States, 39–41; apportionment of, 40–41; forms of, 40–41; in Western Europe, 41; potential for growth of in United States, 76 ff.
Leisure time, international comparative statistics on, 60–63
Leuthold, Jane H., 166
Life expectancy, 4
Living, levels of, 140 ff.
Long, Clarence, 40

MacIver, Robert M., 19
Mack, Ruth, 23
MacKinder, H. J., 6